GULSHAN NASRULLAEVA

PHILOLOGICAL ANALYSIS OF THE TEXT

Editor: Nilufar Rukhillayeva

© Gulshan Nasrullayeva
PHILOLOGICAL ANALYSIS OF THE TEXT
By: Gulshan Nasrullayeva /
Nilufar Rukhillayeva
Edition: February '2024
Publisher:
Taemeer Publications LLC (Michigan, USA / Hyderabad, India)

© Gulshan Nasrullayeva

Book :
PHILOLOGICAL ANALYSIS OF THE TEXT

Author	:	Gulshan Nasrullayeva
Editor	:	Nilufar Rukhillayeva
Publisher	:	Taemeer Publications
Year	:	'2024
Pages	:	230
Title Design	:	*Taemeer Web Design*

INTRODUCTION

Through the science of philological text analysis, students are taught not only the expression of linguistic means in literary texts, but also the philological and linguistic analysis of texts written in different styles. The issue of studying language means in the text and discourse is also discussed. In fact, the main place in the analysis of the text is occupied by the phenomenon of meaning transfer, because any text is not devoid of metaphorical meaning, in this sense, in this training course, any linguistic phenomenon is a multi-style text. and the metaphorical meaning depends on the analysis of the tooth. The textbook discusses the goals and objectives of the science "Philological text analysis", the history of the formation of the science of text analysis, the study of metaphors, types of text, language means in the text and discourse, in particular, the expression of metaphors, phonetic, lexical,

If the language did not have the phenomenon of metaphor, the number of words increased, the expression would not be so impressive and understandable. In metaphor, the economy of language, the power of expressiveness, the power of influence, the ability to accumulate, the function of classification, the integral manifestation of being, the scale of the manifestation of unity and continuity in it are revealed to an incredible degree. It expresses the past and present, worldview, level, cultural and moral level, ethnic and religious values, lifestyle, development and decline, traditions and spiritual attitudes of native speakers. In general, a metaphor is a systematic representation of the past and present of a nation.

Metaphors are as old as language. Its scientific study began with the first ideas about linguistics and today has risen to the level of metaphorology. As a separate component of semiotics, which studies the possibilities of linguistic expression, it is one of the main problems of linguoculturology, which studies the commonality of language and culture, one of the central issues of linguocognitology, which studies the integrity of language and knowledge. , language and ethnic thinking, as one of the important subjects of ethnolinguistics, which studies culture, oratory and the culture of speech, Metaphor is one of the main themes of the art of the word and poetics.

Metaphor is such a fascinating phenomenon that today it has become the object of study of many related sciences. Linguistics, eloquence and neurolinguistics, cultural studies, ethics, aesthetics, psychology interpret it either as a means of expression, or as an instrument of influence, or as a cultural phenomenon, or as a representative of the quality of a person, or as an indicator of morality. , sometimes as a beauty dress. . Both in computational linguistics, and in modern translation technologies, and in the practice of linguistic algorithmization, metaphorical phenomena act as a rather subtle problem.

For a long time, the role of language as a means of communication was ignored. This is especially true in the former Soviet science, in an era when nationalism and national culture and spirituality, national and ethnic values were shunned, about the incomparable splendor of "sheathing a knife". This strength, awe and possibility is indeed reflected in his metaphorical system.

"PHILOLOGICAL ANALYSIS OF THE TEXT" GOALS AND OBJECTIVES OF SCIENCE AND THE STUDY OF METAPHORS.

Lecture 1

PLAN

1. "Philological text analysis" goals and objectives of science
2. Analysis of the text and the study of metaphors in it
3. Text, discourse and metaphor
4. Text types

The language of a work of art is an extremely complex and unique phenomenon. Linguistics in general in the history of philology has taken different approaches to its study. V. Vinogradov, who has been studying the language of literary works all his life, in his lecture "The Science of the Language of Literary Literature and Its Tasks", speaking about the language of literary literature, used the word "language" has two different meanings, emphasizes the use of the word, that is: 1) in the meaning of "speech" or "text" (analysis material for the history of the literary language, historical grammar and lexicology), reflecting the system of a particular national language; 2) "language of art" in the sense of a system of means of artistic expression. No one has ever denied the fact that literature is the art of the word, and its primary element is language.

The great enlightened writer Abdurauf Fitrat wrote in his "Instruction on Literary Rules": "If the commodity (material) in the visual arts is sound, melody, then the visual arts is musical; if there are colors, lines, it will be a picture; stone or other various minerals will be sculpture; if it is stone, wood, brick, stone, earth, then it will be architecture; and the actions of the body and face (torments, facial expressions) are games (tanas); speech, and the word is literature" and defines literature as follows: "Literature is a thought that describes the waves in our feelings with the help of words and sentences, and creates the same waves in others"[1].

The well-known Uzbek literary critic O.Sharafiddinov in the article "Literature begins with language" writes: "Just as there is no fine art without color, music without melody, so there is no literature without language. Literature is called the humanities. writer "Studying different human characters, he discovers important truths that help the development of society. But all this is realized in literature through language."[2].

Here, the following remarks by the great writer and literary critic P. Kadyrov are especially noteworthy: "statues made of copper and marble, buildings made of brick, glass and steel. In a literary work, instead of copper, marble, steel and brick, an artistic word is used. The difference between a literary work and music, painting and other areas of creativity is that its tones are created not through lines and colors, but through words. Therefore, artistic language is one of the main indicators that determine the specification of any literary work. The theory of artistic language is in the first row of questions related to the theory of literature.

In Uzbek linguistics, it can be noted that in the works devoted to the study of the language of works of art, the leading place was occupied mainly by two directions.[3].

1. Linguistic direction. The language of literary and artistic works of that period is studied with the aim of scientific research of

---

[1] Fitrat A. Selected Works. Volume IV. -Tashkent: Spirituality, 2006. -B. 12-13.
[2] Sharafiddinov O. Literature begins with language // Literature and art of Uzbekistan, September 5, 1986.
[3] Donierov H., Mirzaev S. The Art of the Word.- Tashkent: Ozadabi Nahsr, 1962.- 173-174.

the characteristics, lexical, phonetic and grammatical features of the language in a certain historical period, common and different sides with the modern state of the language. In this case, the language of works of art and written monuments serves only as material for research with the same purpose.

This way of describing and researching the history of a language has survived as the oldest and most enduring linguistic tradition. In Uzbek linguistics, a lot of research has been carried out in this direction.

2. Linguistic and poetic direction. The main goal of studying the language of a work of art in the linguo-poetic direction, of course, is different. At the moment, the problem boils down to the fact that the language has different functions. In modern literature on linguistics, four or five functions of language are noted. 1. Communicative task - language is the main means of communication between people. 2. Expressive task - the task of expressing different thoughts and feelings. 3. Constructive task – thoughts the task of forming, organizing and defining the style of the utterance. 4. Accumulative task - the task of collecting and storing social experience and knowledge.

Along with the term "expressive function" of language, in works devoted to the study of language, such terms as "poetic function of language", "artistic function of language" and "aesthetic function of language" are also used. artistic works. But it should also be said that the term "aesthetic function of language" is used quite often in philological literature. This is natural, since the concept of an aesthetic task can generalize a number of concepts, such as expressiveness, artistry, and poetics. In other words, the scope of the concept of an aesthetic task is much broader than these concepts. Of course, other functions of language are realized in any work of art, but the aesthetic function comes first, comes to the fore.[4] Here it should be emphasized that the area of manifestation of this unique aesthetic function of language is only the text of a work of art, and it is also reasonable to believe that language cannot realize this function in any form of speech. In this sense, the following remarks of the linguist D.N.Shmelev are noteworthy: "This function (aesthetic function) of language is manifested not only in a work of art. Whenever our attention is focused on the form of a sentence, on how a thought is expressed, we fall within the scope of this task.

The scientist specifically pointed out that the aesthetic function of language manifests itself in its original form, when the speaker begins to pay attention to the external form of his speech and evaluate the possibilities of linguistic expression. This feature of the language comes into play as soon as the user considers it important not only what to express, but also how to express this "what". The linguistic sign is unique in its artistic and expressive capabilities even in the case of a lively conversation, a lot of sharp jokes in the process of everyday communication, anecdotal laughter, deeply meaningful words, imitation of someone, etc. It is noted that the aesthetic function of the language is clearly demonstrated[5].

The second, linguistic and poetic, direction in the study of the language of a work of art is aimed at studying the same aesthetic function of language. It should be said that the main manifestation of the aesthetic function of language is the text of a work of art, therefore, it is difficult to study the specifics of this function only within the framework of linguistics or only literary criticism. To do

---

[4] Gorelikova M.I., Magomedova D.M. Linguistic analysis of a literary text.– M: Russian language.
[5] Yuldoshev M., Isakov Z., Heydarov Sh. Linguistic analysis of literary text. - Tashkent: National Library of Uzbekistan named after Alisher Navoi, 2010.

this, literary scholars such as literary theory, literary history, poetics and linguistic stylistics, language history, lexicology, semasiology, etymology, grammar must work together. The question of the aesthetic function of language is a complex issue between two major disciplines.

This methodological manual solves such problems as determining the level of reflection of the writer's skill in using language units in a literary text, studying the literary text and its specific features and, on this basis, developing students' skills to perceive linguistic and poetic features in a literary text.

After all, there is no need to prove that the ability to correctly analyze and interpret a literary text is important for the general cultural level of a person, his spiritual and educational maturity, the potential for understanding the world, and the development of emotional and aesthetic perception.

General information about the course "Philological text analysis": "The main goal of the course "Linguistic Analysis of a Literary Text" should be to evaluate the text as a linguo-poetic whole based on the definition of the artistic meaning and artistic content of a literary text. Linguistic analysis of a literary text should be carried out on the basis of special principles. Poetic actualization in a literary text occurs in each of the phonographic, lexical, morphological and syntactic means in its own way. The nature of a literary text as a linguistic and aesthetic whole arises due to the presence of integrative relations that have both formal and semantic essence.

The purpose and objectives of the science "Philological analysis of the text": Students get acquainted with the text, its types and units; introduce the literary text and the types of its content, the expression of intertextuality in a literary text, the means of forming a literary text, the phonographic, lexical, morphological and syntactic features of a literary text, as well as the principles of linguistic and poetic analysis, as well as the theoretical knowledge gained in this course of study, to try linguistic analysis of the best works of art in Uzbek literature.

Requirements for mastering the subject "Philological text analysis": After mastering this subject, students should have a correct understanding of the text and its full language definition, types and units; acquire theoretical knowledge about a literary text and the types of its content, the expression of intertextuality in a literary text, the means of forming a literary text, the mechanisms for the emergence of an aesthetic goal, manifested through language units; the acquisition of practical skills in determining the phonographic, lexical, morphological and syntactic features of a literary text; they must be able to independently analyze a certain work of art on the basis of the principles of linguistic and poetic analysis.

The connection of the science "Philological analysis of the text" with other sciences. The content of this course is closely related to such subjects as linguistics, literary criticism, textual criticism, culture of speech, stylistics, philosophy, ethics, aesthetics, logic and psychology. Linguistic analysis of literary text

requires a serious philological preparation from the student. Because a literary text, as a product of creative thinking, is an artistic and aesthetic whole that is very complex in form and content.

Recommendations for organizing and conducting the educational process "Philological text analysis": Brainstorming, decision tree, boomerang, "3 in 1" (three in one), forum, conclusion, scientific discussion, "workshop", "linguo poet", "message" can be used directly in the process of linguistic analysis of a literary text. interactive technologies are used. When studying each topic, innovative methods are introduced, taking into account its specific features.

Methodical instructions: Each topic must be studied thoroughly. Theoretical questions and assignments on the topic should be carried out under the supervision of a teacher. Familiarization with basic and additional literature, their independent study and assimilation by students should be strictly controlled. At the beginning of the course, each student should be given the task of reading a specific work of art and preparing for a linguistic analysis. The student searches for and collects examples on each topic discussed in the lecture from his chosen works of art and brings them to the state of a written test.

It is necessary to provide the student with detailed information about the use of scientific and theoretical literature, articles and dictionaries, the order and rules for citing them.

Text description. In the scientific literature, the term "text" is interpreted in different ways. The explanatory dictionary of the Uzbek language indicates that the word "text" is borrowed from the Arabic language, is an old book word and is equal to the meaning of the word "text". In this dictionary, the word text is defined as follows: [r<lat] 1. A written, copied or printed creative, scientific work, speech, document, etc., or a fragment thereof; text. Article text. 2. A poem, a word that underlies a piece of music, for example, a melody, opera, romance, etc. 3. The name of one of the large fonts in printing. Therefore, when we speak a text, only the written form should be taken into account. The same emphasis was kept in the updated explanatory dictionary: text [Arabic - shoulder; written expression of

speech, text] 1. Author's work or document, in written or printed form. 2. The main part of the printed edition without drawings, drawings and comments. First of all, it should be said that, since communication between people is carried out through texts, limiting the text to only the written form contradicts the rules of the existing theory of the text. After all, it is unimaginable that any communication between people will take place only and only in writing. It has always been recognized that the basic unit of syntax is the sentence, and the fact that the text or its units should be considered higher syntactic-communicative units than the sentence has become one of the basic rules of modern text linguistics. Therefore, only what is reflected in the letter is considered speech. Of course, there is no need to prove that it is wrong to say that a sentence in oral speech cannot be a sentence. If only all written speech is called a text, then logic requires that a sentence be recognized only in written form. But of course this is impossible. True, no one denies that oral speech exists only during speech, and written speech is not limited in time, but this means that it is generally impossible to remember, store in memory, restore it or its individual parts. , this is wrong. The suggestion that a text is created only when complete oral speech is translated into writing is tantamount to saying that the water flowing in a river is not water, but that this "substance" becomes water only when it is poured into bottle. In modern linguistics, the text is treated as a separate large unit of language (supra-syntactic unit) and the main object of the field called text linguistics.

This is written by the linguist M.Kh.Khakimov: "In the dictionary meaning of the word text, the existence of the concepts of connection and connection, therefore, the study of the connection of textual content with the help of some connecting elements is one of the main problems. area "Linguistics of the text". In this paper, the author emphasizes that the term "text" should be distinguished from other linguistic terms such as "speech", "context". In addition, the term "discourse" is also widely used in most works devoted to the study of text problems in world linguistics. Although the term is widely used in such fields of science as literary criticism, sociology, political science, philosophy, logic and psychology, along with text linguistics, it has a single, widely recognized interpretation in text linguistics itself. It has no meaning and is used to express various concepts. Initially, the terms "discourse" and "text" were used to refer to the same concept, later "text" was used to refer to written communication, and "discourse" to refer to oral communication. The meaning of this word is French discourse - "speech", "to speak".

Metaphor. Aristotle defines it as: "the transfer of the meaning of a word from genus to species, from species to genus, or from species to species, or on the basis of alternation."[6]. In addition, Aristotle states that "... to create good metaphors is to draw analogies."[7]. Some scientists who disagree with this opinion (A. Richards) "every speaker has experience in using metaphor, Aristotle's opinion that this skill is not available to everyone does not justify itself, a person acquires the ability to speak using the example of other speakers, naturally, he also learns the experience of using metaphors directly, commenting" metaphor - the art of managing life "-gives an estimate that[8].

---

[6]Aristotle. Poetics. - L.: 1927. - P.39.
[7]Aristotle. Hair. in 4 vols., so-called. IV. M., 1983. Also: Ivor A. Richards. Rhetoric of Philosophy. The article is in the following collection: Cassirer E., R. Jacobson, A. Richards, M. Black, Dj Searle, A. Vejbitska, A. Ortoni, J. Lakoff, N. Goodman, i dr. The theory is metaphorical. - M.: Progress, 1990. - P.58. URL::http://fileshare3200.depositfiles.com/auth-13415932567aa0fa1b3be3cc9a4042fa-13.206.39.161-2033652370-119224315-guest/FS320-2/153998.doc
[8]Ivor A. Richards.Rhetoric of Philosophy. The article is in the following collection: Cassirer E., R. Richards, M. Black, Dj Searle, A. Vejbitska, A. Ortoni, J. Lakoff, N. Goodman, i dr. The theory is metaphorical. - M.: Progress, 1990. - P.58. URL::http://fileshare3200.depositfiles.com/auth-13415932567aa0fa1b3be3cc9a4042fa-213.206.39.161-2033652370-119224315-guest/FS320-2/153998.doc?

In his time, the comparative theory of the study of metaphor was criticized by J.Searle and M. Black. J.Searle stated that the metaphor depends on the influence or opposition of two semantic meanings of the verbal, i.e. metaphorical expression and the actual contextual environment.[9]. M.Black was one of the first in science to define a metaphor as "a creation, not an expression of comparison."[10].

This has prompted many researchers to explore semantic relatedness. They also argued that metaphors create comparisons rather than revealing them, i.e. metaphors show similarities between two things that no one had thought of before.

Traditional views of metaphor have regarded metaphor as a mere linguistic unit, a contextual growth, without taking into account its function of facilitating the exchange of ideas. However, the thought itself has a metaphorical character, it manifests itself through comparison and finds its expression in the language.

Scientist I.M.Sechenov, who first studied the psycholinguistic nature of metaphor, proved the process of turning human emotions into symbols by purely physiological factors.[11] Aspects of the subject related to logic, memory, imagination and language are Gregory,[12] G. Leibniz[13], Rubinstein,[14] Shilkov,[15] Piaget[16] Feuchtwanger,[17] P.Sartre[18], Shcherba[19], Potebnya,[20] Vinogradov,[21] Ivlev[22], G.Frege,[23] C.Pierce[24],

---

[9]Sir J. Metaphor // Theory of Metaphor. - M.: Progress, 1990.
[10]Cherny M. Metaphor // Theory of Metaphor. - M.: Progress, 1990.
[11]Sechenov I.M. Selected philosophical and psychological works. - M.: Ogiz, 1947.
[12] Gregory R.L. Eye and brain, psychology of visual perception. - M.: Progress, 1970.

[14]Rubinshtein S.L. Being and consciousness (On the place of the mental in the universal connection of the phenomena of the material world). - M.: AN SSSR, 1957.
[15]Shilkov Yu.M. Gnoseological principles of thinking. - St. Petersburg: Publishing house of St. Petersburg State University, 1992.
[16]Piaget J. Selected psychological works. -M., Enlightenment, 1969.
[17]Feuchtwanger L. Sobr. hair v 6 up to max. T. 6, book. 1. M., Fiction, 1990.

[20]Potebnya A.A. Thought and language. - Kharkov: Peaceful Labor, 1913.
[21]Vinogradov V.V. History is the word. - M.: Tolk, 1994.

Wittgenstein,[25] Humboldt[26] and found expression in the studies of others.

Based on the existing aspects of teaching, research has been conducted on the analysis of metaphors in language. As a result, the study of metaphor has gone beyond the interdisciplinary system, and important research has gradually emerged that focuses on the study of metaphors in the language of science. The phenomenon of metaphor has been of interest to researchers for many years, focusing on its nominative nature and aesthetic potential. Most of the created studies are devoted to various aspects of metaphorology, however, the variety of approaches to understanding the essence of metaphor is due to the fact that this phenomenon has ambiguous aspects and the need to study it still exists. Metaphor is currently of interest to linguists, literary critics, cognitive scientists, neuropsychologists and other scientists. Today in the world Russian,

The problem of studying poetic metaphor is also not new, more and more researchers are turning to individual language formations, so the question of the functioning of metaphor in idiolect sounds each time takes on a new look. In modern linguistics, there are several priority areas for the analysis of metaphorical images: cognitive, linguoculturological, conceptual, and others. At present, most of the scientific works of the educational plan are devoted to the analysis of the linguistic personality of politicians, the description of political metaphors. In this regard, E.V. There are studies by Budaev, N. Karaulov, E. S. Khrabrova, A.P.Chudinov and others. Within the school of cogitology, there are not many works devoted to the study of

---

[23]Frege G., On the concept and the object. In: Translation from the philosophical writings of Gottlob Frege. Ed. Peter Geach and Max Black, Basil Blackwell, Oxford, 1980.
[24]
[25]Wittgenstein L., Philosophical research. Trance. GEM Anscombe, The Macmillan Company, New York, 1953.
[26]Humboldt V. Selected Works on Linguistics. - M.: Progress, 1984; Humboldt V. Culture of language and philosophy. - M.: Progress, 1985.

poetic metaphor. In this regard, the studies of T.I.Chubaeva, N.S.Trifonova, I.V.Tolochin and others are of great importance. Today, the object of analysis of metaphorical activity are poetic texts of different periods. It has been studied from ancient times to the present day. Similar studies can be found in the works of E.F.Volodarskaya, E.Kh.Volodarskaya Ryadchikova, S.A.Akhmadeeva, A.B. Barykin, E. P. Kislova, K.A.Turanina and many other linguists also dealt with the problem of metaphor .

The study of metaphor in the context of sciences has led to the emergence of new knowledge, technologies and methods in various areas of research within the framework of the study. Recent theories are linked to the scientific interests and efforts of neurophysiologists, linguists, and even physicists such as J.R.Tolkien's neural theory.[27]

In this dissertation, anthropomorphic metaphor is considered in a cognitive aspect: a linguistic personality that performs cognitive and emotional-evaluative functions is considered as a unit of a phrase. The anthropomorphic definition is used to denote such metaphors as one of the prototypes (a set of source or target areas) expressing the field of concepts related to the understanding of human nature.

It is worth paying attention to the opinion of F. I. Tyutchev that the choice of a linguistic person is not accidental for us. F.I.Tyutchev claims that this is an excellent example of a combination of two types of linguistic figures: poetic and political texts. Although the political personality of Fyodor Tyutchev is not as pronounced in his lyrics as the personality of the poet (Tyutchev is a politician, he appears mainly in letters and journalism), his influence in a poetic context cannot be completely excluded. This feature was noted by many researchers: M. Yu. Lotman and, in recent years, F. I. Tyutchev, despite the presence

---

[27] Metaphor, by which I live / Metaphors We Live Author: Dj. Lakoff, M. Johnson. M.: Editorial URSS, 2004.-. 256 pages

of various works on the language of poetry, D.Tilman, D.D.Sedova, E.S.Sklyar, M.V.Marshina, N.V.Atamanova, A.L.Golovanevsky, I.O.Klyueva, a special study of poetic cognitive metaphor in its systemic form is excluded from the point of view of the Tyutchevids.

By the 1930s, the English linguist A.A.Richards proposed calling the constituent metaphors the names "content, essence" and "shell, imagery (image)". In his conclusions, A. A. Richards called a metaphor an organic phenomenon that arises in the process of interaction of conceptual structures located on deeper layers than language combinations and existing at the base of words.[28].

G. N. Sklyarevskaya notes that in the 60s and 70s of the 20th century metaphor was studied in four directions - nominative-objective, formal-logical, psychological and linguistic, and notes that these studies have formed eleven independent directions in recent years.[29]

In addition to this classification, three main stages of development in the history of the artistic and philosophical interpretation of metaphor can be indicated: 1) the interpretation of metaphor as a special type of comparison; 2) interactive concept; its representatives believe that the collision of different levels of meanings in linguistic means creates a special context that allows you to take a fresh look at all objects; 3) the concept of "semantic turn", the development of new ways of seeing the world as a result of the collision of various "linguistic worldviews" that form the cultural landscape of the language[30].

---

[28] **A. A. Richards.** Rhetoric of Philosophy. The theory is metaphorical. - M., 1990. - p. 44-67.
[29] **Sklyarevskaya** G. N. Metaphor and systemic language. SPb., 1993.
[30] Link taken from this source: Enikeev A. A. Metaphor and theory of literature and philosophical discourse. Problems of philology, cultural studies and art history in the light of modern research. collection of materials of the XVIII International Scientific and Practical Conference. - Makhachkala, June 19, 2016 See: Enikeev A.A. The space of the cultural landscape: traditions and modern interpretations // Actual problems of modern social and humanitarian knowledge. Materials of the IX All-Russian Scientific and Practical Conference. - Nizhny Tagil: NTGSPI, 2015, -p.41-47.

O.A.Svirepo also describes three main mechanisms of metaphor and its occurrence: 1) semantic (Black, Richards, Rothbart, etc.); 2) pragmatic (Cohen, Marglit, Schibles, Lakoff and Johnson); 3) notes that he was researched in the semiotic (Henle) direction[31].

As noted, the study and study of metaphor in world linguistics is determined based on the classification of the Russian linguist O.Laguta: 1.Ancient metaphorology (Aristotle, Philodem, Theophrastus, Cicero, Quintilian); 2. edieval[32] metaphorology (Isidore of Seville, Bede the Venerable, George Hirobosk, Philip Melanchthon); 3. Metaphorology of a new era; 4. Metaphorology of the twentieth century: new aspects of the object of study, such as the definition of its boundaries.

However, human organs and other related phenomena may cause migration later. For example, the eye first began to represent the human organ of vision, and then other similar objects found in nature. The eye of a ring, the eye of a needle, the eye of a spring, etc. Prior to this study in the Uzbek language, devoted to the study of anthropomorphism, scientific texts were practically not analyzed. Recognized mainly in literary texts. In order to fully identify anthropomorphic metaphors and their specific features, it is necessary to analyze texts of different styles from linguistic, sociolinguistic and linguoculturological points of view. Also, learning to use comparative anthropomorphic metaphors will allow you to better understand it. Anthropomorphic metaphor - a person and what belongs to him (part of the body,[33] For example, Yu.M.Aleksandrova,

---

[31] Svirepo O. A. Metaphor as a code of culture. Abstract diss. blood philosophical science. - Rostov-on-Don, 2002. http://www.dissercat.com/content/metafora-kak-kod-culture

[32] *O.mediéval refers to the Middle Ages.

[33] Khohamkulov A. On the classification of metaphor in the Uzbek language. Collection of scientific articles dedicated to the 20th anniversary of the independence of the Republic of Uzbekistan. Linguist. 2 books. – T.: Akademnashr, 2011. – B. 85–88.

Yu.V.Gorshunov emphasize that a distinctive feature of the works of J. Durrell is the ability to give vivid descriptions of animals, using the specific features of the image of people by imitating the animal world by human society.[34]

Against the general background of the described anthropomorphic metaphors, there are metaphors based on the exploitation of insects (fleas, beetles and flies), reflecting the professional and social characteristics of human life, created on the basis of comparing animals with people of a certain profession. and status. It can be said that anthropomorphic metaphors are the most common type of metaphors.

The study of metaphors in world linguistics. In the world, the active use of metaphors not only in literary texts, but also in other areas has been scientifically widely studied. The spectrum of anthropomorphic metaphors and comparisons depicted by society reflects the professional characteristics of human life. According to one writer, businessmen, fishermen, warriors, hairdressers, dancers, musicians, singers and other professions can also be compared. Comparison is usually based on the natural coloration of the animal, which is similar to the same work clothes of a certain profession, or similar to such habits as the usual actions and behavior of people of any profession and social status. The interaction between man and animals attracts the attention of many authors. One of the favorite stylistic devices used by writers to describe human interaction with the natural world, is an anthropomorphic metaphor based on the transfer of human qualities to animals. It uses an extended interpretation of the anthropomorphic metaphor, which makes it possible to generalize various cases of the transfer to an animal of

---

[34] **Alexandrova** Yu.M., Gorshunov Yu.V. Author's metaphors and comparisons based on the image of a dog in the work of Gerald Durrell // Bulletin of the Bashkir University. 2016. Vol. 21. No. 3. - p. 698-705.

human qualities associated with anthropomorphic features (appearance, physical characteristics, behavior, character traits, way of thinking, way of life, etc.). Anthropomorphic metaphor is a "mirror image" of zoomorphic metaphor. When we talk about animals, we mean a wide variety of representatives of the animal world, including mammals, birds, reptiles, amphibians, fish, insects and others. it is based on the transfer of human qualities to animals. It uses an extended interpretation of the anthropomorphic metaphor, which makes it possible to generalize various cases of the transfer to an animal of human qualities associated with anthropomorphic features (appearance, physical characteristics, behavior, character traits, way of thinking, way of life, etc.). Anthropomorphic metaphor is a "mirror image" of zoomorphic metaphor. When we talk about animals, we mean a wide variety of representatives of the animal world, including mammals, birds, reptiles, amphibians, fish, insects and others. it is based on the transfer of human qualities to animals. It uses an extended interpretation of the anthropomorphic metaphor, which makes it possible to generalize various cases of the transfer to an animal of human qualities associated with anthropomorphic features (appearance, physical characteristics, behavior, character traits, way of thinking, way of life, etc.). Anthropomorphic metaphor is a "mirror image" of zoomorphic metaphor. When we talk about animals, we mean a wide variety of representatives of the animal world, including mammals, birds, reptiles, amphibians, fish, insects and others. allows us to generalize different cases of the transfer of human qualities to an animal, depending on the way of thinking, lifestyle, etc.). Anthropomorphic metaphor is a "mirror image" of zoomorphic metaphor. When we talk about animals, we mean a wide variety of representatives of the animal world, including mammals, birds, reptiles, amphibians, fish, insects and others. allows us to generalize different cases of the transfer of human qualities to an animal, depending on the way of thinking, lifestyle, etc.). Anthropomorphic metaphor is a "mirror image" of zoomorphic metaphor.

For example, in world linguistics, one can single out many studies on the analysis of literary texts, including researchers J. Based on the analysis of metaphor in Darrell's work, he encounters a wide range of images created by[35]. Durrell's anthropomorphic metaphors are usually based on the author's attitude to being when expressing situations, feelings, experiences, and fantasies. Some researchers have studied anthropomorphic metaphors that reflect the professional and social characteristics of human life, created on the basis of comparing animals with certain professions. The comparison is based on the natural color of the animal, which is the same or similar to work clothes or habits similar to the usual actions of people of any profession or social status.[36]. I.A.Arzhanova[37] in his article focuses on the functions of anthropomorphic metaphor in the English-language economic discourse.

According to him, the present time covers the issues of research of such stylistically expressive devices as anthropomorphic metaphors in the English-language economic discourse. An analysis of anthropomorphic metaphors with a communicative-functional meaning of speech - this has significantly expanded the list of basic functions and types of anthropomorphic metaphor. Economic concepts, like those related to other areas of human activity, can be

---

[35] Aleksandrova Yu. M., Gorshunov Yu. V. Conceptual metaphor "man - life" and produced by Gerald Durrell // In the world of science and art: issues of philology, art history and cultural studies: collection of articles. articles based on the materials of the XXXII International Scientific and Practical Conference. Novosibirsk, 2014. No. 1 (32). pp. 57-62.
[36] Yu.M. Aleksandrova, Yu.V. Gorshunov Anthropomorphic metaphors reflecting the professional and social specificity of a person // Humanitarian Sciences Series. 2017. S-22
[37] https://cyberleninka.ru/article/n/funktsii-antropomorfnoy-metafory-v-angloyazychnom-ekonomicheskom-diskurse/viewer

expressed by various means of expression, and this happens much more often than it seems at first glance. The most popular and productive stylistic unit here is the metaphor. Thanks to metaphor, simple and complex economic phenomena can be clearly and figuratively described. The presence of a metaphor in the text allows the recipient to understand that the author puts something else into the word that is not related to its dictionary meaning.

1) the recipient's awareness that this statement is not verbatim and that its misinterpretation may disrupt successful communication;

2) the recipient is trying to associate the metaphor with a number of object variants;

3) the recipient finds among the possible values the one that best suits the given context and situation.[38]

Recent studies in the field of cognitive linguistics have shown that since ancient times, the human language landscape has been recreated with words.

E. S. Abramova[39] Modern Russian media discourse reflects the path of social changes, spiritual, moral and ideological research that Russian society has gone through over the past ten years. Media speech is understood as a social priority principle for understanding and interpreting socially significant meanings in the media, as well as a social regulatory mechanism that controls public consciousness by creating and multiplying socially significant meanings and assessments in the media.

The focus of this study is the concept that reflects the nature of the movement of dominant meanings and their linguistic

---

[38] Arzhanova I.A. Functional approach and interrogative training in adequate metaphorical and theoretical-practical translation // Integration of education. 2013. No. 2. S. 136-142.
[39] http://www.rusnauka.com/17_PMN_2014/Philologia/9_172101.doc.htm

objectification in the context of changes in public consciousness under the influence of internal and external factors in the process of comprehending the cultural space of society.

In the modern socio-cultural context, Rodina magazine is of particular importance and relevance as one of the most serious, intellectual and prestigious scientific and educational periodicals aimed at comprehending the cultural, spiritual and moral foundations of Russian society, its present day and its role. in the history of human civilization.

A. V. Myasnikova[40], a metaphor by E.V.Alikina, one of the most common tropes, has attracted the attention of scientists and cultural figures since ancient times. The study of metaphor began with Aristotle, whose works were summarized thanks to his followers.[41] A.Richards, M.Black, N.D.Arutyunova, M.Johnson, J.Well-known linguists such as Lakoff and others had a great influence on the study of metaphor, its place and role in language.

In connection with the dominant role of the anthropocentric approach to language in modern linguistics, much attention is paid to the study of anthropomorphic metaphors in the term systems of various fields of science. On the one hand, we are dealing with a term whose invariable features are one-sidedness, fullness, accessibility, stylistic neutrality, contextual independence, and metaphor implies the presence of figurativeness, figurativeness, expressiveness, emotionality.

Arutyunova N.D.[42], many linguists, such as S.G.Dudetskaya, I.V.Pashkova, E.E.Pimenova and N.O.Samarkina, emphasize that

---

[40] https://lektsii.org/12-47199.html
[41] Aristotle. Poetics: patience. hair v 4 tomax: T.4 / Aristotle. - M.: Publishing House Thought, 1983. - 830 p.

[42] Arutyunova, N.D. Metaphor and discourse / N.D. Arutyunova // Theory of metaphor / General. ed. N.D. Arutyunova, M.A. Yurinskiy. - M.: Progress, 1990. - S. 5-32.

anthropomorphic metaphors play an important role in the construction of conceptual and verbal systems of a person, in the classification of the environment, as well as in the processes of thinking and perception.

Professor of Baku State University Sevinj Maharramova: "As you know, metaphor is based on comparison. A person can compare the unknown with the known, and this manifests his attitude to objective reality. Since time immemorial, metaphorization has been applied primarily to words denoting the most familiar concepts and objects from the immediate environment of a person.[43] It says that.

The metaphorical view of the man-made world is inherently anthropocentric. Just as God created man in his own image, so man metaphorically creates reality in the form of a particular likeness of his body and its constituent organs, his physiological and other physical needs, his genetic and other connections with his relatives.[44] Some literature also uses the term "physiological metaphor". Chudinov notes that the physiological metaphor is widely used in the content of the headlines of Russian newspapers, and in the last decade of the 20th century and the beginning of the 21st century, the physiological metaphor was actively used, as in previous periods.[45]

He also stated that human activity gives its subjects the closest and most understandable characteristics, as a result of which reality appears in the form of a human body, with its physiology and anatomy. Like a living organism, the subjects of activity act as creatures with an emotional-volitional sphere, capable of experiencing

---

[43] https://gisap.eu/ru/node/7709
[44] Chudinov, A.P. Political linguistics: a study guide / A.P. Chudinov. - Yekaterinburg: Ural Publishing House. Mister. ped. Univ., 2003. - S. 77.

[45] Chudinov, A.P. Political linguistics: a study guide / A.P. Chudinov. - Yekaterinburg: Ural Publishing House. Mister. ped. Univ., 2003. - S. 78.

and expressing emotions. Like a living organism, subjects of activity have the ability to cognize and can perform operations related to thinking, analysis, conclusions, etc.[46]

This has been extensively researched in Uzbek linguistics, and the following example can be given: / Morning opens its eyes and melts, / Cycads cry for joy / Smallpox smiles for joy / Flowers bathe in the wind (Hamid Olimjon "Chimyon Esdalikari").

Reflecting on the cognitive nature of anthropomorphic metaphor in artistic speech, it should be noted that representatives of the cognitive approach to the study of J. Lakoff and M. Johnson indicate a person's tendency to metaphorical perception of the surrounding reality[47].

The identification of nature with man is considered natural, based on the cognitive nature of the metaphorical transfer. The metaphor goes beyond the literal representation of external reality: the images of nature are seen through the human essence at the level of mental and physical characteristics. The similarity of natural phenomena and objects with a person characterizes the artistic proposal, which makes it possible to identify and interpret the features of metaphorical migration. The resulting associative connection between nature and man is born and develops by combining additional linguistic knowledge (ie, knowledge about the context and situation) and the recipient's ideas about the world around. In modern studies, it is believed that the metaphor reveals its potential only in a certain context; context is "the semantic substance

---

[46]Chudinov, A.P. Political linguistics: a study guide / A.P. Chudinov. - Yekaterinburg: Ural Publishing House. Mister. ped. Univ., 2003. - S. 78.

[47]Lakoff, J. Metaphors that I live by: a study guide / Dj. Lakoff, M. Johnson. - M.: Publishing house of URSS scientific and educational literature, 1990. - S. 387–415.

of metaphor", i.e. surrounding words explain the metaphor[48]. "Speech should be understood as "the creation of real speech, a clear cognitive process associated with the creation of speech, and the text is the end result of the process of speech activity, leading to a certain fixed form," says Kubryakova.[49]

Animals in general and the relationship of man to nature are expressed in a peculiar way by poets in a figurative form. For example, in the following poem, the word wolf is used to refer to a person:

The thick branches glisten / The sunbeams rest affectionately, / The double gun on the shoulder - / The man entered the forest... / The thick branches are drowned / The bloody light of the day / The shotgun on his shoulder, the wolf comes out of the forest...(Sh. Rahman)

At the beginning of the poem, the poet begins the story of a man entering the forest, but in the last stanza "... with a gun on his shoulder, a wolf comes out of the forest."

In the history of Uzbek culture there was a period of worship of animals and birds. As a result of the traditions of mystical thinking left over from the period of animal totemization, there are still cases of taking people's names from the names of animals: Wolf, Eagle, Leopard. Although they are based on metonymy (i.e., transferred on the basis of the relation of a generic name to a person), it is certain that metaphorical models worked behind the secondary meaning of the term. In addition, intention and dream, based on unrealistic similarity, also cause the emergence of names based on the folk-mental essence, based on a metaphorical model, based on the names

---

[48]Sklyarevskaya, G. N. Metaphor in the language system: textbook /G. N. Sklyarevskaya. - St. Petersburg: Nauka Publishing House, 1993. - S. 35.

[49]

of animals: 1. "Wolf (self.) - according to ancient custom, passing through the jaw (skin) of a wolf to make healthy and strong a child born with a tooth removed. Forms: Boriboy, Borijon, Boribek, Boritoy, Borikul.[50] 2. "Tiger (self.) - grow up bold and bold, like a tiger, or a child born in the month of Assad (July)."[51]

In human life, agriculture is on the same level with cattle breeding. Therefore, the culture of agriculture is widely reflected in the language. The role of agricultural culture in the anthropocentric metaphor is unique and varied. "The presence or absence of words of one type or another in a particular language, a lot of them or, conversely, few, depends on the objective needs of people who speak the language. Such a need is determined by the natural environment, economic and social conditions, spiritual and cultural needs of this people. For example, the Uzbek language has many terms related to agriculture, aquaculture and other professions. In the language of the peoples living in the Far North, there are many words and terms associated with snow and cold, reindeer herding and fishing.[52]The same points can be made in relation to the metaphorical layer of the vocabulary of the language, the system of metaphorically significant expressions and means.

Thus, the basic rules for the use of metaphor in speech were understood, the concept of metaphor as a language unit was defined. Metaphor as a linguistic phenomenon accompanies language and speech everywhere; many linguists consider metaphor from different positions and give their own definitions of this phenomenon. In this work, more attention was paid to the opinion of A.P. Chudinov, who defines metaphor as the main mental process that combines two

---

[50]Begmatov E. Uzbek names. Tashkent: "National Encyclopedia of Uzbekistan" GNIZ, 1998. (- 608 p.) - P.82.
[51]Begmatov E. Uzbek names. - V.545.
[52]Begmatov E. Lexical layers of the modern Uzbek literary language. - Tashkent: Science, 1985. - P.33.

conceptual fields and allows you to use the power of constructing the original field with the help of a new field.

The study of metaphors in Uzbek linguistics. Uzbek linguistics also has a number of studies on the study of metaphors, which are a means of a deeper understanding of the world. For example, U.S. Gabulova considers metaphor to be a literary innovation and distinguishes it from comparison (tashbeh) by the absence of comparison.[53]. Using metaphor as an alternative to metaphor[54] the result of the views existing in the scientific and literary heritage is subject to responsibility. Abdurauf Fitrat, like other literary scholars, showed metaphor as a poetic art.[55]. As in other languages, the study of metaphors in Uzbek linguistics received serious research development by the last decades of the 20th century.

The scientist M. M. Mirtozhiev, who conducted multifaceted research on Uzbek lexicology, divides metaphors into speech and language phenomena. To the types of metaphors in German linguistics: personification, symbolization, allegory, synesthesia: "These types of metaphors related to speech phenomena can be applied to metaphors related to linguistic phenomena, with some modifications. At the same time, it is necessary to exclude symbolism and allegories arising from the pure nature of speech.[56]. Because symbolization is a metaphor that arises in relation to the ellipsis in speech. And the allegory comes to the surface in the context of speech and intonation. Based on this, metaphors, which are linguistic

---

[53] Obtain USA Correlation of integral and differential symbols in a metaphorical text (on the example of Uzbek folk riddles). Phil, science, name. scientific school. abstract submitted for receipt. - T., 2007.

[54] Obtain USA Correlation of integral and differential symbols in a metaphorical text (on the example of Uzbek folk riddles). Phil, science, name. scientific school. abstract submitted for receipt. - T., 2007; and a glossary of literary terms. - T .: Teacher, 1970.

[55] Obtain USA Correlation of integral and differential symbols in a metaphorical text (on the example of Uzbek folk riddles). Phil, science, name. scientific school. abstract submitted for receipt. - T., 2007.

[56] Mirtozhiev. MM. Semasiology of the Uzbek language. - T .: Mumtoz soz, 2010. - P. 96.

phenomena, are divided into such forms as simple metaphor, personification and synesthesia.[57]reacts.

According to M. M. Mirtozhiev, a simple metaphor cannot be called an almost reduced comparison. Simple metaphor is based on simple comparison, the similarity of referents, while personification is based on the simulation of an inanimate referent to an animate referent; Synesthesia is based on the comparison and imitation of the signs of a referent perceived by one sense organ with a referent perceived by another sense organ.[58]

All of the metaphors mentioned are basically conditional metaphors.[59]The linguist R. Kongurov calls the metaphor a hidden comparison and distinguishes it from a simple comparison: a simple comparison always consists of two main members, while in a metaphor only the second member - the comparison remains, the comparison is removed, but clearly noticeable from the context. So, the object described in the metaphor is perceived through this second member[60]. M. Yuldoshev says that according to the content in linguistics, three types of metaphors are distinguished, i.e. typical metaphors, synesthetic metaphors and revitalization metaphors.[61]N. M. Makhmudov singles out synesthetic metaphors among metaphors and "words in synesthetic metaphors can be mutually contradictory, even completely opposite to each other. Such unusual compounds are also called "oxymoronic compounds" (for example, bitter truth is good, and lies are bad. - E.V.)[62].

---

[57]Mirtozhiev. MM. Semasiology of the Uzbek language. -T.: Mumtoz soz, 2010 -B. 97.
[58]Mirtozhiev M.M. Semasiology of the Uzbek language. -T.: Mumtoz soz, 2010.
[59]Linguistic analysis of a literary text: Methodological guide / M. Yuldoshev, Z. Isakov, Sh. Khaidarov: executive editor Makhmudov N.M. - T .: Publishing house of the National Library of Uzbekistan named after Alisher Navoi, 2010.
[60]Kongirov R. Graphic means of the Uzbek language. -T., 1977.
[61]Yuldoshev M. Secrets of the word shepherd. -T., 2002. S. 73.
[62]Mahmudov N. The culture of the teacher's speech. -T., 2009. 2nd ed., -B. 80.

In particular, D.S. Khudaiberganova uses a new, modern approach to the study of metaphors. The scientist evaluates metaphors as a phenomenon that manifests aspects specific to the national and cultural thinking of text speakers, along with the acquisition of an important cognitive and semantic value in the text, and says that texts built on the basis of comparisons and metaphors make it possible to determine textual forms cast in one language or another, he evaluates metaphors as precedent forms of text.[63].

In Uzbek linguistics, a group of scientists and researchers interpret revitalization as a special type of metaphor. And L. Dzhalolova sharply distinguishes revitalization from metaphor and interprets it as an independent visual tool. In his opinion, animation is a phenomenon different from metaphor, "in which human actions, feelings, speech, thinking are transferred to inanimate objects, but a person is not understood through them."[64]. On the contrary, M. Mirtozhiev shows revitalization as a meaningful type of metaphor. In our opinion, this opinion expresses scientific truth.

G.K. Gabuljonova, who studied metaphorical movements in the Uzbek language using the method of component analysis, emphasizes that the metaphor cannot be the same for all lexico-semantic groups (LSG). There are also specific name transfer rules: different LSGs are assigned to transfer in different situations. For example, animal names have been moved to reflect a more human nature, and plant names have been moved to reflect appearance. G.K. Gabulzhonova defines the philosophical foundations of metaphorology as follows:

1. Objectivity (everything exists as it is before and after we begin to study it).

---

[63] Khudaiberganova D.S. Anthropocentric interpretation of artistic texts in the Uzbek language. Abstract of a doctoral dissertation. -T., 2015. -B.18.
[64] Gasanov A.A. Linguistics of revitalization in the stories of Abdulla Kahkhor. Scientific world Kazakhstan. 4 (32) 2010. -p.37-38.

2. Substantiality (any object of study, including a linguistic unit, is the sum of its qualities - matter).

3. Accounting for the possibility of intermediate situations between conflicting events[65].

GK Gabulzhonova summarizes the nature of metaphor and views on it in three groups. These are: 1. Metaphor (almost) any way of transferring the name (Arastu, E. Cassirer); 2. Metaphorical reduced comparison (A.A. Potebnya and his followers); 3. Metaphor is a special type of transfer (A.Vezhbitskaya, N.D.Arutyunova and Uzbek linguists).

Sh. Makhmaraimova comprehensively approached the study of metaphor from the linguo-cognitive and linguo-culturological points of view. The scientist analyzed the theoretical views on the mechanism of the emergence of theomorfic metaphor in general, the cognitive patterns of the movement of metaphorical thinking, the functions of reception, processing, storage and transmission (representation) of metaphorical knowledge. The ethnogenesis of theomorfic images, forming the object of theomorfic metaphor under the influence of local mythological systems, was deeply studied on the example of the gradual development of metaphorical thinking, and through this sharp difference from religious metaphor, the position was relatively first explained by the spelling of names that name theomorfic images, and the synthesis of images, related to the object of theomorfic metaphor and religious metaphor, gave clear conclusions about the mechanism of occurrence, as well as on the materials of world literature translated into the Uzbek language, theomorfic metaphors with a high frequency of discursive use are highlighted, which explains the "cliche" function of theomorfic

---

[65]Kabulzhonova G. Systematic linguistic interpretation of metaphor. Candidate of Philology. The dissertation abstract is written for receiving. -T., 2000.

metaphors in typical communicative situations, expressing the national-mental, communicative expression of the owner of the language in a typical communicative situation; theoretically proved that theomorphic metaphors, which have the quality of moral and evaluative psycho-psychic unity, occupy their rightful place in the national linguo-cognitive picture of the world, and expressed their attitude towards them as linguistic cultures. explains the "cliché" function of theomorphic metaphors expressing communicative expression in typical communicative situations; theoretically proved that theomorphic metaphors, which have the quality of moral and evaluative psycho-psychic unity, take their rightful place in the national linguocognitive picture of the world, and expressed their attitude towards them as linguocultures. explains the "cliché" function of theomorphic metaphors expressing communicative expression in typical communicative situations; theoretically proved that theomorphic metaphors, which have the quality of moral and evaluative psycho-psychic unity, occupy their rightful place in the national linguo-cognitive picture of the world, and expressed their attitude towards them as linguistic cultures.[66]

However, although anthropocentric research is carried out in linguistics, the anthropomorphic type of metaphors is not specifically studied. The study of anthropomorphic metaphors in connection with various discourses is of great scientific, theoretical and practical importance.

---

[66]Makhmaraimova Sh. Cognitive aspect of theomorphic metaphor in the national language picture of the world. - Tashkent. 2018. 161 p.

The study of metaphors in text and discourse. The secrets of metaphor attracted the greatest thinkers from Aristotle to Hegel, then E. Cassirer, G. O. Gasse and other great thinkers. Much has been written about metaphor. Not only scientists spoke about it, but also its creators - writers, poets, artists and filmmakers. There is no critic who does not have his own opinion about the nature and aesthetic value of metaphor. The study of metaphor is traditional, but it would be a mistake to think that it is supported only by the strength of tradition. Philosophy, logic, psychology, psychoanalysis, literary criticism, fine art theory, semiotics, rhetoric, linguistic philosophy, various schools of linguistics - on the contrary, it is becoming more powerful and expanding rapidly. Interest in metaphor contributed to the interconnection of these areas of scientific thinking, their ideological consolidation, as a result, the formation of a science of knowledge, which studies various aspects of the human mind. "It is based on the assumption that the structures of human cognition (perception, language, thinking, memory, action) are interconnected within the framework of one common task - the implementation of the processes of assimilation, processing and transformation of knowledge, which essentially determines the essence of human consciousness"[67].

In recent decades, the focus of the study of metaphor has shifted from philology (rhetoric, stylistics, literary criticism) to areas dealing with the analysis and evaluation of poetic metaphor, the study of applied discourse and thinking, cognition and consciousness, and conceptual systems. and finally, artificial intelligence modeling.[68]. The

---

[67] Petrov VV Language and logical theory: in search of a new paradigm. - "Issues of Linguistics", 1988, No. 2, p. 41. See also Sat: New about foreign linguistics, vol. XXIII: Cognitive aspects of language. M., 1988.
[68] senior bibliography of W. Shibles' work on metaphor (Shibles W. Metaphor: Annotated bibliography and history. Whitewater - Wisconsin, 1971), consisting almost entirely of philological studies, with a fairly complete bibliography, placed in Sat. Theorie der Metapher (brs. von A. Haverkamp. Darmstadt, 1983)

metaphor was considered as the key to understanding the foundations of thinking and the processes of creating not only national-specific thinking about the world, but also its universal image. Metaphor strengthened the connection with logic on the one hand and mythology on the other.

The growth of theoretical interest in metaphor was stimulated by its growing presence in various types of texts, from poetic discourse and journalism to language in various fields of scientific knowledge. Naturally, the spread of the metaphor to different discourses was not considered. Art critics, philosophers and psychologists, scientists and linguists are increasingly turning to the problem of metaphor. The reliance on metaphor has significantly expanded the "material base" of this study: there are studies of metaphors in various terminological systems, children's speech and didactic literature, various media, advertising language, product names, headlines, sports, aphasic speech, and even the deaf. and silent speech was[69].

The spread of metaphor in many genres of artistic, everyday and scientific speech forced the authors to pay attention to the utilitarian advantages it provides, and not to the aesthetic value of the metaphor. R. Hoffman, the author of a number of metaphor studies, wrote: "This metaphor is very practical. ... It can be used as a descriptive and explanatory tool in any field: in psychotherapeutic conversations and conversations between airline pilots, in ritual dances and programming languages, in art education and in quantum mechanics. Metaphor, wherever it occurs, always enriches our understanding of human action, knowledge and language.[70].

---

[69] Metaphor in language and text. Articles in collections: M., 1988; Metaphor and thought. Cambridge, 1979; Metaphor: problems and prospects. Brighton, 1982; The omnipresence of metaphor: metaphor in language and thought. Amsterdam - Philadelphia, 1985.

[70] Hoffman R. Some consequences of metaphor for the philosophy and psychology of science. - In the book: The omnipresence of metaphor. Amsterdam, 1985, p. 327.

Along with the aforementioned positive effect, it has been suggested that the power, influence, and thickness of the metaphor led to some negative consequences. The idea of the omnipresence of metaphor has pushed into the background the problem of its limited application in various discourses. This led to the blurring of the boundaries of the very concept of metaphor: a metaphor is any way of indirect and figurative expression of the meaning contained in a literary text and fine arts - painting, cinema, theater. Less attention has been paid to the distinction between metaphor and metaphor used as a nominative device, which redoubles the idea of different object classes. Metaphor as style and metaphor as ideology are analyzed together in many studies.

Below we will consider the role of metaphor in practical (everyday and working), scientific and artistic speech, among semiotic concepts and in the system of roads.

In practical speech, we are not talking about the obvious meaning of the metaphor, but about its inconsistency, clumsiness and even disproportion in a number of functional styles. Thus, despite the semantic possibilities of metaphor, it has no place in the telegram language, its text is built on brevity, and not on the basis of metaphorization.

In laws and military orders, regulations, orders, decrees and punishments, any requirements, rules of conduct and safety, circulars, instructions and medical recommendations, programs and plans, litigation (sentences and private orders), expert opinions, comments, patents and petitions , wills, patents and promises, notices and warnings, ultimatums and proposals, requests - in a word, everything that must be strictly observed, executed and controlled, clearly and distinctly understood. The above list shows that metaphor does not correspond to the prescriptive and commissive functions of speech. Naturally, the metaphor rarely occurs in questions expressing the requirement of the recipe.

They imply not only feasibility, but also the possibility to determine the degree of deviation of the prescription and the degree of responsibility for the deviation. Metaphor prevents this. However, when the center of gravity is emotional impact, metaphor is prohibited. Thus, the requirement of everyday speech becomes a threat aimed at intimidation, which can be expressed metaphorically. The commonality of the goal naturally gives rise to the commonality of the language means used. The field of expression of emotion and emotional tension introduces an element of artistry with metaphor into everyday speech.[71]. In the Uzbek language, texts involving metaphors are mainly found in the form of address:

Nodirajan, Shoirajan,

my body is not moving

from distant oases

my mountains *call*

the sky is full of air

just not enough for me.

Nadirajan, Shoirajan, my body does not move, there are drops of tears in my eyes, the streams do not wash away. Nadirajan, Shairajan, my body does not move, this salty river on my forehead... the air filled with the sky is not enough for me. Nadirajan, Shairajan, my body does not move, go to the snowy mountains: say that the poet is lying in God's courtyard... Air full of heaven is not enough for me alone... (Sh. Rahman. Chosen). The highlighted units are used figuratively.

---

[71] Teliya V.N. Metaphor as a model of meaning production and its expressive and evaluative function. - In the book: Metaphor in language and text. M., 1988.

The sense of intuitive similarity plays a large role in practical thinking that determines human behavior and cannot be reflected in everyday speech. This is the inevitable and inexhaustible source of the metaphor "in everyday life." Figurative thinking is very important in life practice. A person is able not only to identify individual objects (in particular, to recognize people), but also to establish similarities between areas perceived by different senses (the phenomenon of synesthesia: hard metal and hard sound, warm air and warm tone), but also concrete and abstract things, matter and spirit, gaining a commonality with each other (water flows, life flows, time flows, thoughts flow, etc.).

The properties of sensory mechanisms and their interaction with the psyche allow a person to make incomparable comparisons and unchanging measurements. This device is constantly moving and creates a metaphor in any conversation. Entering into everyday speech, the metaphor is quickly erased and included in the common vocabulary of the language. But the use of developing living metaphors leads to limitations with the functional-stylistic and communicative features of speech discussed above. However, they are not the only ones who can stop the metaphor. Metaphor generally does not fit well with the main components of the sentence - its subject and predicate - tasks performed in practical speech.

In everyday speech, metaphor has no place in any of these functions. Its essence does not correspond to the purpose of the main components of the proposal. The metaphor of the defining function performed by the subject (more broadly, the specific referential members of the sentence) is very conditional, it cannot be fully related to the subject of speech. The metaphor of an object intended to introduce new information is a very vague, semantic phenomenon.

Arutyunova says that sooner or later practical speech will kill the metaphor. Its figurativeness does not agree well with the tasks of the main components of the sentence. Its vagueness does not correspond to the communicative goals of the main speech acts - there is no connection between a conscious request and information, a prescription and an obligation.[72].

This is not to say that metaphor is not needed for practical speech. Every innovation, every development starts with a creative effort. This is as true for life as it is for language. The act of metaphor-creation underlies many semantic processes - the development of synonymic means, the emergence of new meanings and their defects, the creation of polysemy, the development of terminological and emotional-expressive vocabulary systems. Without metaphor, there would be no vocabulary of "invisible worlds" (inner life of a person), a zone of secondary predicates, that is, predicates expressing abstract concepts. Then there would be no predicates of broad compatibility and predicates of fine semantics (for example, the use of action verbs)[73]. Metaphor reveals one of the paradoxes of life, the immediate goal of action (and especially creative action) is often opposite to its long-term results: the desire for concrete and individual, subtle and figurative, metaphor can only make language erasable and impersonal, general and general. By creating an image and appealing to the imagination, the metaphor reveals the meaning perceived by the mind.

Natural language can extract meaning from an image. The result of the process of metaphorization, which ultimately destroys the metaphor, are the categories of linguistic semantics. The study of

---

[72] N. D. Arutyunova Theory Metaphor. - M., 1990. - S. 5-32

[73] Stepanov Yu. S. V three-dimensional spatial language. M., 1985, p. 229

metaphor allows us to see the raw material that makes up the meaning of a word. As a result, the mechanism of action of the considered metaphor leads to the conventionalization of meaning. He defines the role of metaphor in the development of the semantic style and brings it into the sphere of interests of linguistics.

Consider now the place of metaphor in scientific discourse. The relationship between scientific terminology and the use of metaphor in a theoretical text varied depending on many factors - the philosophical views of various authors, the assessment of scientific methodology, the role assigned to it in the general context of the scientific and cultural life of Russia. society, in particular, the role assigned to it by intuition and thinking by analogy, the nature of the scientific field, the opinion about the language, its essence and purpose, and, finally, it is necessary to dwell on the nature of metaphor[74].

Naturally, a sharp division between the intellectual and aesthetic activities of man, science and art, the desire to distinguish between solid knowledge and myth and religion, and epistemology - faith, has always been against the use of metaphors in the language of science.

English rationalist philosophers had a negative attitude towards metaphor. So, according to T. Hobbes, speech primarily serves to express thoughts and transfer knowledge, and words used in the literal sense correspond to this function, because in metaphors and in general in figurative meanings one can see only confirmation of the meaning of words that perform the main purpose of language , said it would be an obstacle to[75]. He also wrote: "The product of human thought is understandable words, cleared of all ambiguity by precise definitions. Thinking is the step, the growth of knowledge is the path,

---

[74] Gusev S. S. Science and metaphor. L., 1984. -S. 54.
[75] Hobbs T. Leviathan. M., 1936, p. 62.

and the welfare of mankind is the goal. On the other hand, there are such things as metaphors and vague words, and to think in them is to walk among many absurdities, and the result of them can be discord, anger or hatred.[76].

J. Locke in his argument against the imperfection of the language "only inspires false ideas, excites passions and thereby confuses the mind, and therefore is essentially a pure lie. ... if people enjoy being deceived, it's pointless to complain about the art of deception[77].

These estimates are based on the fact that metaphor is one of the most convenient and effective means of expressing the meaning that exists along with the use of words in a direct and concrete sense. This unites thinkers who adhere to rationalistic, positivist and pragmatic views, supporters of the philosophy of logical analysis, empiricists and logical positivists. In these areas, metaphor is considered inappropriate in scientific work, and "creating a metaphor" is equated with committing a crime.

Philosophers and scientists of the romantic type, who sought the origin of language in the emotional and poetic impulses of man, on the contrary, considered metaphor to be a fatal inevitability, the only way not only to express a thought, but also to think about oneself. . F. is especially strict and consistent in this regard. We will focus on Nietzsche's statements. Nietzsche writes: "the thing-in-itself" (which would be pure, non-finite truth) is completely unattainable ... for the creator of language, in his opinion, it is absolutely not worth looking for. He only expresses the relations of things to people and uses the most vivid metaphors to express them. Nervous excitement becomes an image! First metaphor. Image becomes sound! Second metaphor.

---
[76]Ibid., p. 63
[77] Locke J. Hair. in 3 vols., so-called. 1. M., 1985, p. 567.

And each time there is a complete jump into a completely different and alien world ... When we talk about trees, we think that things know nothing about themselves, nor about colors, neither about snow, nor about flowers; in fact, only metaphors allow us to vividly understand their true essence.[78]

A worldview built from clear anthropomorphic ideas cannot be anything other than "a multiplied trace of one prototype - man." It is impossible to affirm a concept that does not generate its metaphor. The path of truth is blocked. "What is true? A moving mass of metaphors, metonymy, anthropomorphisms - in a word, the sum of human relations ...; truths are illusions that have forgotten what they are, metaphors that have become something terrifying"[79].

There can also be an aesthetic relationship between subject and object, expressed only in metaphor. Therefore, it is natural for a person to strive for conscious knowledge of metaphor. He strives to realize all new possibilities and finds them in myth and art. Man destroys "a huge system of concepts." He "scatters the fragments, ironically collects them again, connects the most alien in pairs and separates the most related; by which he shows that he is guided by intuition, and not by concepts.[80].

Thus, according to Nietzsche, knowledge is fundamentally metaphorical, aesthetic in nature and does not operate with the concept of verifiability. If rationalism rejected metaphor as a low and unnecessary form of expressing truth, then philosophical irrationalism sought to give metaphor the whole world of knowledge, extracting truth from it. Various variants and concepts of such an approach to the role of metaphor in cognition exist in all philosophical

---

[78] Nietzsche F. On Truth and Lies in an Extramoral Sense (1873). - Nietzsche F. Poland. patience hair., vol. 1. M., 1912, p. 396
[79] That source. 399 pages
[80] That source. 405 pp.

concepts marked by subjectivism, anthropocentrism, intuitionism, interest in mythopoetic thinking, and national images of the world.

H. Gasset believes that metaphor is almost the only way to define objects at a high level, inseparable from content. It is later said to provide "epistemic access" to the concept of metaphor.[81]. Considering metaphorical models of consciousness, Gasset wrote: "Our understanding of the world depends on our ideas about consciousness, which, in turn, determine our ethics, our politics, our art. It seems that the whole universe is a huge building, full of life, which rests on the metaphors of a small and airy existence. This is especially true of anthropomorphic metaphors.

E. Cassirer began to publish a series of studies of symbolic forms in human culture. In the short book "Language and Myth" that preceded the publication of this work, Cassirer summarized in a concise form the basic rules of his concept.[82]. This collection also includes the final chapter of the book titled "The Power of Metaphor". E. Cassirer expanded the field of title theory by studying pre-rational thinking related to language, mythology, religion and art. Cassirer, it became necessary to study the unity of the human mind, which combines various mental activities, their genesis and general structure. Epistemic research, according to Cassirer, should not begin with an analysis of the forms of cognition, but with a search for primary, prehistoric forms of the origin of human ideas about the world that are not based on the categories of reason. According to Tilda Cassirer, both logical and mythological forms of thought are expressed. He was looking for reflexes of the mythological vision of the world in a metaphor, which he understood very broadly (Cassirer also included metonymy and synecdoche in this concept).

---

[81] Boyd R. Metaphor and Change in Theory. - In the book: Metaphor and thought. Cambridge, 1979
[82] Cassirer E. Philosophy of Symbolic Forms. bd. 1 - 3. Berlin, 1923-1929

The symbolism found in language, mythology, art, religion, logic, mathematics, etc., gives the researcher access to consciousness. The ability to symbolically represent categories of content is characteristic of man, unlike animals. The cashier's attention is focused on the symbols.

Unlike Nietzsche, Cassirer did not reduce all ways of thinking to metaphors. He distinguished two types of mental activity: metaphorical (mythopoetic) and discursive-logical thinking. The discursive-logical path of the concept consists of a sequence of step-by-step transitions from a certain state to ever wider classes. Taking some empirical property of the object as its starting point, thought works its way through the entire realm of existence (hence the term "discursive thinking") until it is convinced of the desired concept. This is how natural science concepts are formed. Their goal is to turn the "rhapsody of feelings" into a code of laws.

Unlike discursive thinking, the metaphorical "study of the world" (that is, mythological and linguistic, Cassirer considers them together) has the opposite direction: it reduces understanding to a point, to a center. If discursive thinking is broad, then mythological and linguistic representation of reality is strong; if the first is characterized by a quantitative parameter, then the other two are qualitative.

As a result, Nietzsche's voice that he distrusts metaphor and all human knowledge became a hope for its uaristic potential, for its suggestiveness. From the idea that the metaphor is embodied in thinking, a new assessment of its cognitive function arose. Emphasis was placed on the modeling role of metaphor: a metaphor not only forms an idea about an object, but also determines the way and style of thinking about it. A special role in this belongs to the main metaphors, which define analogies and associations between different systems of concepts and create more specific metaphors. Previously, (basic) metaphors, which mainly attracted the attention of ethnographers and culturologists studying national-specific images of the world, in recent decades have entered the sphere of interest close to the psychology of expert thinking and the methodology of science. A significant contribution to the development of this problem was made by the works of M. Johnson and R. R. Tolkien, J. Lakoff. This collection includes chapters from their book Metaphors We Live In.

The author of the theory of frames M. Minsky (scenarios in the context of the study of the subject and event objects) also introduces comparisons based on basic metaphors into his system. He writes: "Such analogies sometimes allow us to see an object or idea in the "light" of another object or idea, which allows us to apply knowledge and experience in one area to solve problems in another. Thus, knowledge spreads from one scientific paradigm to another ... Thus, we are accustomed to considering gases and liquids as particles, aggregates of particles, waves and surfaces of wave propagation fields"[83]. According to Minsky, metaphor contributes to the formation of unpredictable inter-frame relationships that have great heuristic power. So, the key metaphors connect the image of one part of reality with another part of it. They give their concept in comparison with the already established system of concepts. Since the time of Marx, it has become customary to represent society as a concrete building, structure[84]. This metaphor allows you to highlight the basis (foundation), various structures (infrastructures, superstructures), supports, blocks, hierarchical levels in society. Society is viewed in

---

[83] Minsky M. Wit and logic of the cognitive unconscious. - In: New in foreign linguistics, vol. XXIII, p. 291 - 292.
[84] Althusser L. Lear le Capital. Paris, 1968

terms of construction, growth, destruction, and fundamental changes in society are interpreted as its reconstruction.

Linguists know metaphors that give the key to understanding the nature of language and its units: the biological understanding of language has made it natural to liken it to a living and developing organism that is born and dies (living and dead languages); comparativists offered metaphors for language families and linguistic kinship (the proto-language acted as a pratenitor); the main metaphor of structural linguistics was hierarchical structure; for generativists, a metaphor for language as a generative device. A change in the scientific paradigm is always accompanied by a change in the basic metaphor, which creates a new field of comparison, a new analogy.

Metaphor is incompatible with many parameters of practical and scientific discourse. At the same time, it is used both in everyday life and in science. Metaphor corresponds to the expressive-emotional function of practical speech. However, another source is more important: the metaphor corresponds to the ability of a person to capture and create analogies between different classes of persons and objects. This ability plays a big role in both practical and theoretical thinking. This feeling is a common stimulus for both practical and scientific discourse to generate metaphors. In both cases, the metaphor marks only the beginning of the thought process. There can be no comparisons or conclusions here. The wave theory of light was not designed to treat light as a wave. The metaphor that gave impetus to the development of thought is fading away. It's a tool not a product of scientific research. Thus, giving impetus to the semantic process in practical speech,

Poetic (figurative) thinking is limited to the initial stage of cognition. At the same time, the creation of an image in art, including a metaphorical image, determines the creative process. Artistic thinking does not begin with an image, but is built on it. Metaphor is both a tool and a fruit of poetic thought. It corresponds to the literary text in its essence and content.

Although it is superfluous to talk about metaphor in relation to the visual arts, nevertheless, it is not useless to touch on this topic. This leads to the question of the place of metaphor in a number of other semiotic concepts, in particular, of its relation to a symbol.

Metaphor and symbol based on image[85]. The image is the source of basic semiotic concepts, and its structure is created by the interaction of fundamentally different planes (organic or traditional) - the plane of expression (signifier) and the plane of content (signaling). Both metaphor and symbol are often defined by reference to an image. Most critics are vague about metaphor and symbolism in the individual style of this or that poet. You can find synonymous uses of the expressions metaphorical image and symbolic image. In fact, the concepts of metaphor and symbol are closely related. Their relationship, based on a number of common features, is reinforced by the general tendency of literary criticism to expand the use of terms. Meanwhile, metaphor and symbol cannot be defined in terms of their position in the hierarchy of semiotic concepts.

Returning to this source, the concepts of image, metaphor and the symbol inherited from it have a number of common features that distinguish them from the central semiotic concept - the sign. Metaphor and symbol, like the image, arise by themselves in the process of artistic development of the world. They are relatively independent of human will. Their meaning cannot be fully formed.

---

[85] Arutyunova N.D. The word is a symbol. - In the book: Thinking, Cognition, Artificial Intelligence. M., 1988. -S. 54.

Both metaphor and symbol are objects of interpretation, not understanding.

This feature does not allow them to serve as a means of communication: neither symbols nor metaphors convey messages. They cannot order or commit. They are unaddressed. This distinguishes them from the sign. With a gesture, you can perform a speech act: greet and say goodbye, invite people to let in or out, threaten or warn. Neither a symbol nor a metaphor can be included in contexts in which a nominal sign is equivalent to an utterance with a communicative purpose (illocutionary force). The concept of a sign is connected with the pragmatics of speech. A sign is a tool in the hands of a person. With the help of symbols, they communicate and regulate interpersonal relationships.

Starting with an image, a metaphor and a symbol, develop it in different directions. The metaphor is based on a categorical change that drowns its image. In turn, this is facilitated not by the referential aspect of the word, but by the predicative position, which emphasizes semantically. Therefore, the metaphor gradually becomes understandable and relies on the meaning that can enter the lexical fund of the language. For a symbol that is not characterized by its use in an object, on the contrary, the form stabilizes. The dictionary of symbols created by P. A. Florensky consists of the names of geometric figures, and the only article written by him for this dictionary is devoted to this issue.[86].

The metaphor preserves the integrity of the image, which can fade into the background, but does not fall apart. The symbol behaves differently. As a result of the general tendency to simplify the image, symbolic meaning can be obtained from a special feature of the image

---

[86] Nekrasova E.A. The unfulfilled vision of the 1920s for the creation of the "Symbolarium" (a dictionary of symbols) and its first edition "Point". - In the book: Monument culture. New discoveries - 1982. L., -S. 198.

- its color, shape, position in space. The decomposition of the image into symbolic elements makes it possible to read it. The image becomes "text". Although symbols (like metaphors) are independent of each other, they can be integrated into a single system. Color symbols can form their own "language" (code). In this case, the interpretation of symbols approaches their understanding based on knowledge of the code. This situation is typical for iconography (more broadly, ritual symbolism).

The schematization of the signifier in the sign makes its connection with the meaning less organic. This fundamentally distinguishes a symbol from a metaphor, in which the relationship between the image and its meaning never reaches full convention.

The development of a metaphor in the direction of determining the meaning that performs a characteristic task determines its involvement in an objective position. Of course, in the language of poetry, where all positions are semantically saturated and do not require explication, there are no strict positional restrictions in metaphor. Text can be entered in its secondary function, i.e. the naming function. And in everyday speech, its use can interfere with the understanding of the message: - I saw a nightingale among the crows, about five or ten lousy zagks with their heads down, salinity so that hearts are torn and dying, a lot of tips are woven about the nightingale. (Shaukat Rahman). An appeal to a metaphor is usually carried out by establishing an anaphoric connection of the subject with a direct noun.

A symbol, unlike a metaphor, acts as a symbol rather than a description, reinforcing its meaning. Symbols cannot replace an item. They indicate the meaning, but do not apply it to the description of another ("foreign") object. They are not distinguished by the vagueness of the metaphor.

This difference also leads to a difference between the typical meanings of a symbol and a metaphor. Metaphor has no semantic restrictions. Performing a characterizing function in a sentence, a metaphor can have any characteristic meaning, ranging from figurative (provided that bright semantic ambiguity is preserved) and ending with the meaning of a wide area of relevance. At the same time, the metaphor usually refers to a specific object, and this keeps it within the meanings that are directly or indirectly related to reality. A symbol, on the contrary, easily overcomes "gravity". He seeks to express the eternal and difficult, which is considered non-conceptual real truth in teachings with a mystical bent.

The great spirit and great memory of the world can only be called symbols. Therefore, the symbol often has vague transcendental meanings. "Revelation, silence and speech are hidden in the symbol." Metaphor also has another, more "worldly" function. It is designed to create an image of an object that reveals its essence. The metaphor deepens the understanding of reality, the symbol takes it beyond its limits.

The anthropomorphic metaphor represents the linguistic meanings attached to the figurative shell of the vehicle, and the symbol to general ideas. So the symbols are random[87] cannot represent, and talking about the general ideas expressed in art and its images almost automatically turns these symbols into symbols. Therefore, he talked extensively about the ideological content of "Lison ut tire" in this aspect.

---

[87] Stepanov Yu. S. V three-dimensional spatial language. M., 1985, -S. 72.

There is another way to turn an image into a symbol in the context of art. In this case, we are talking about the choice of the main image or the main metaphor in the work. If the metaphor develops with semantic impoverishment and at the same time with greater certainty, then the symbol, which contains the ideological meaning of the entire work, on the contrary, expands its content, but at the same time does not make it completely clear. The symbol enriches the image with the ability to metonymically represent the whole as a part.

In addition to the above, there is another fundamental difference between metaphor and symbol. The transition from image to metaphor arises from semantic, i.e., sociolinguistic needs and concerns, while the transition to a symbol is often determined by extralinguistic factors. This applies to intermittent and constant characters. The image is found in the life of a person (personal symbol), society, state, religious or cultural community, ideological community, family life and, finally, in the life of all mankind. A metaphor, however subjective, cannot be a metaphor for "someone". It does not belong to any personal or social sphere. The symbol belongs to the private sphere, but it is not created by the individual.

If images are added, they become symbols, rise, grow. Such word usage, characteristic of a nominal symbol, shows that the symbol performs a far from simple function in a person's life. It is no coincidence that groups of people are marked with social symbols, the purpose of which is to unite and direct the efforts of the group.[88]. However, the semantic interpretation of state, tribal and national symbols can be very ambiguous and even unstable: the "strength" of a symbol distorts its meaning.

---

[88] For a review of the literature on this topic, see: Firth R. Symbols public and private. London, 1973. -p.66.

The characterization of the relationship of metaphor to poetic speech will be incomplete if we do not briefly touch on the question of the role of metaphor in a number of other tropes, and above all in direct systemic relations. These include simile, metamorphosis, and metonymy. The comparison is based on reference cases in which the features of each path are most pronounced.

The proximity to the metaphor of figurative comparison is beyond doubt. Comparative (same, exactly as, similar) or similar,[89] Avoiding predicate comparisons is often the primary method of constructing metaphors. The consequence of this action is a significant change in the syntactic structure. The comparison becomes a noun, or rather, a taxonomic pretext: this girl looks like a doll → this girl looks like a doll → this girl is a real doll. Therefore, the formal and semantic differences between figurative comparison and metaphor are largely related to the difference between these two types of logical relations.

In combination with predicates of different meanings, comparison is characterized by freedom, denoting those actions, states and aspects of the object that stimulate comparison:

Gazelle written on the waves of the river, /

Grass bends over and reads a book. /

A moment of joy and laughter, /

*The sun will sigh for a moment (R.P.)*like

R. Parfi became everyone's favorite creator, because he was able to use all the possibilities of his native language. In particular, it is noticeable that he uses metaphors effectively:

The reeds whisper by the river, /.

White clouds in the blue.

---

[89] Turovsky VV How, fuck, remember, creative comparisons: interpretations for a group of quasi-synonyms. - In: Handbook and Problems of Text Education. M., 1988. -S.74.

There is a living grace in the world, /

Someone announces, asks. /(Same source, p. 24.)

In the stanzas of the poem, it is sometimes possessive, sometimes complementary, sometimes inverted. All the verses in this paragraph are metaphorical. From the beginning of the stanza "The reeds are joking," the reader feels a mood characteristic of poetry. This is the expressive power of metaphor.

Substantive metaphor lacks syntactic mobility. It does not appear in refinement, refinement, or verbose modifiers. This context is entered by the creator.

Since the metaphor is compact, it easily falls into the "narrowness of poetic categories" (Tinyanov). He avoids modifiers, explanations and reasons. Metaphor shortens speech, and comparison expands it. These tropes correspond to different tendencies of poetic language.

The transition to the category of taxonomic predicates determines the semantic specificity of the metaphor: if the comparison sees the similarity of one object to another, regardless of whether it is permanent or transient, real or apparent, limited to one aspect or globally, then the metaphor reveals a stable similarity that reveals the essence of the subject and, in ultimately, its permanent nature. Therefore, metaphorical statements do not allow conditions of time and place. On the contrary, the comparison is very characteristic of the limited time or a certain episode: at that moment he was like an angry tiger. The similarity may be illusory. Metaphor is an argument about the impression of similarity. The debate about the choice of metaphor is about the true nature of the subject. You can say that today I feel like a bird.

In particular, it strictly does not allow the metaphor to manifest the property that created the similarity: the metaphor itself occupies a syntactic place intended for the explication of the base of comparison, that is, the place of the predicate.

The semantic mechanism of a metaphor includes four components, partially expressed in its surface structure: the main and auxiliary subjects of the metaphor explain some of the properties of each.

In the figurative-meaningful anthropomorphic metaphor, the term of comparison (auxiliary object), its characteristic (or features), as well as the main object for the speaker to turn to the metaphor, the characteristic of search are synthesized. It is formed by the intersection of the properties of two objects.

In the metaphor with the subject, the auxiliary subject class is not indicated, it is an adjective. This is also a mandatory sentence - the main subject marker. When words are said to be prickly, the adjective prickly indicates both the auxiliary object (it is a piercing weapon) and the desired property of words: it is the ability to affect the soul of such a person, produced by a sharp point that pierces a living body.

Finally, one can understand the conciseness of the metaphor, its "shorthand". Reducing the "comparison sign" (a bunch of comparison), the metaphor also exteriorizes the basis of comparison. If in the classical case the comparison is three terms (A is similar to B based on S), then the metaphor is usually two terms (A B).

Along with the base of comparison, the metaphor also rejects all modifiers. The metaphor is figurative, but does not describe the specifics. Along with modifiers, it also removes all possible explanations from itself. A metaphor is a judgment, an inference without a motive. It is semantically rich but not precise. If we remember that metaphor is also a contrast, from which the first term is excluded, then we can fully appreciate the extent to which it is based on rejection and choice - the two main principles of the poetic word, in which motives, explanations, distributors are rejected, "background" etc. are covered only by the uniqueness and possible accuracy of choice. Metaphor is centripetal, but it has centrifugal forces created by semantic radiation.

If we allow this phenomenon to be seen as a qualitatively different form of speech, metaphor can be opposed not only to comparison, but also to metamorphosis. V. V. Vinogradov wrote about the need to distinguish between metaphor and metamorphosis: "In metaphor there is not even a shadow of thought about the transformation of an object. On the contrary, the "double", only the verbal identification of one "object" with another - a sharp opposition - is an integral part of the metaphor. As a result, it is necessary to distinguish from metaphors and comparisons in the correct sense the semantic connection with the object (with its objects), the means of its animation, the predicative creative state that reveals its figurative background.[90]. There are many unique examples of metaphor in the lines of Usman Azim: I was so wounded: My trunk is crooked, / My flowers are awe that does not fill the heart. / Nobody's love fell on my fruit, / My leaf is an umbrella that cannot be used by ants. / Before goodbye! I've reached the goal, / Gardeners, further along the road, where ... / Again: He walks laughing. He can't cry./ He puts his hand on his chest. His hand is covered in blood. / He shouts to me: "My friend, do not be afraid, stop, / Dawn! The dawn is in my chest."/ Laughs. Dawn is not a father, / He is generous. He gives his life to the

---

[90] Vinogradov V.V. A poem by Anna Akhmatova. - Quote. according to the book: Vinogradov V. V. Poetics of Russian literature. M., 1976, p. 411.

world. / My friend, I have a question, take a breath, / Friend, what to do with the morning when the sun is buried? /(Elections, p. 16)

V. Vinogradov says: "in these cases ... we are dealing not only with verbal metaphors, but also with echoes of "mythological thinking". All these "changes" are considered by the hero as a reality. Therefore, we are not talking about linguistic metamorphoses, but about a way of perceiving the world.[91].

Indeed, a metaphor, which is a means of characterizing an object, always retains its focus on it. In it, concreteness (the main subject of metaphor) "survives" in its objectivity, and the term of comparison (auxiliary subject) eventually becomes a property value. On the contrary, in creative metamorphoses the main theme disappears, but its "bud" remains. It is no coincidence that the creative predicate is in the imperative after the verbs to appear, demand, introduce, see, bypass, appear, etc. Metamorphosis clearly "shows", "twirls":

In autumn... the earth moved, /

The soil is dry in autumn. /

Then suddenly the leaves lit up red, /

*They are red and then the leaves burn. (Cholpon, Khazan, p. 156.)*metaphor drives the entire development of the plot.

Entry into the realm of semantics is characteristic of metaphor, but not of metamorphosis, which is "a special contingency of substances."[92]referring to the language is not suitable as a special way of converting and creating values. However, there is also a metamorphosis in semantics, which reveals a connection with the action of the subject. With this approach, the name is adverbialized

---

[91] Vinogradov V.V. A poem by Anna Akhmatova. - Quote. according to the book: Vinogradov V. V. Poetics of Russian literature. M., 1976, p. 412.
[92] Potebnya A. A. From notes on Russian grammar. M., 1958, especially p. 485.

and acquires a new meaning. In this case, we are thinking of metaphor, not metamorphosis.

At the "intersection" of metaphor and metamorphosis, an auto-metaphor arises - the metaphorical self-identification of the poet, shedding some light on the psychology of creativity.

As noted above, metaphor emphasizes the essential and therefore permanent nature of the object, while simile and especially metamorphosis focus on temporal similarity or episodic "change". The poet is distinguished by an abundance of images:

Endless snow melted

/the old earth is abandoned again./

Giant plums in the valley/

it bloomed white in one night./

White clouds have landed on the ground,/

Have miracles happened? /

Oh what a wonderful night /

valley planted with white torches./(Sh. Rahman). However, a direct connection of metaphors is also used here.

At the same time, the poet often emphasizes the situation that corresponds to his nature. At this point, the whole poem moves towards this mood. Sh. Rahman: Green tree in Subhidam/

he pressed his face against my window,

to glass level

/softly wrote flowers./

A rustling breeze blew, /

foaming with haste and joy,/

Spring, the body opens and shines, /

overcome by the mist of spirits./

As if the sun had split...

Happiness drowns the world./

I don't melt every spring

a tree that teaches to live.

Briefly, the relationship of metaphor to metonymy should be touched upon, this difference is clearly shown by R. Jacobson, who connects the differences in the behavior of aphasics with a violation of the syntagmatic and paradigmatic mechanisms of speech organization.

If the relationship between comparison, metaphor and metamorphosis, which occupies a predicative position in a sentence, can be characterized paradigmatically, then metaphor and metonymy are positionally distributed and have a syntagmatic connection with each other. Metonymy gravitates towards the position of the subject sentence and other members of the address. Not used in a predicate. Metaphor, on the other hand, is closely related to the position of the predicate in its main function. This distribution comes from the nature of each trace. Metonymy, paying attention to the peculiarity of individualization, allows the addressee of the speech to identify the object, distinguish it from the observed field, distinguish it from other objects that exist with it, and the metaphor gives the object an important characteristic.

For example: Love is a beautiful butterfly, / I'm afraid that I caught salinity. / A butterfly next to me when I was chasing it, / I don't remember what I did. / My heart is like an offended child / no fun, no consolation. / Love is a beautiful butterfly, / It sits on flowers anyway. / I run after it. , / I will be ashamed of the cave / - no matter how much I run, I will stay behind in salinity. /

The above passage shows that metonymy and metaphor also differ in patterns of semantic correspondence. Metonymy is intended to identify the whole with its characteristic part. Therefore, it is logical to take definitions related to this part, and not to the whole. At the same time, the predicate and the definitions derived from it are consistent with the referent of the "whole", that is, with metonymy: Love is a beautiful butterfly still landing on flowers. At this point the flower and the flower are in a menonymic state, although the poet used a strong metaphor, but in most poems love is described as tied to a butterfly.

The emergence of metaphor, that is, the realization of semantic consistency through the whole sentence (or even through the entire poetic text) turns the metaphor into an image (as a special artistic device).[93]. Metaphor is the opposite of metonymy when it falls into the position of the subject. The definition of a metaphor can describe its true denotation, and the predicate corresponds to the false denotation (auxiliary subject) of the metaphor.

Dual address - the identity of the addressee and his identity as the recipient of speech - receives both metaphor and metonymy. In the first case, it is close to the original meaning: love is a beautiful butterfly. Out of context, ambiguous events can be interpreted in two ways, which can be understood as metonymy, and Love is a beautiful butterfly / yet sitting on flowers. / It is correct to understand it as a metaphor, in our opinion.

Metaphor performs a characteristic function in a sentence and is mainly focused on the position of the predicate. The characteristic function is carried out through the meaning of the word. Metonymy acts as an identifier in a sentence, metaphor is primarily the transfer

---

[93] Hegel. Lectures on aesthetics. - Hegel. Works, vol. 1, p. XII, M. 1938, p. 416-418.

of meaning, metonymy is the transfer of reference. Metaphor and metonymy are considered in a syntagmatic aspect - they can exist together in a sentence. The contrast is related to each other. Metaphor, considered socio-paradigmatically, is opposed to comparison and metamorphosis, based on the presence/absence of identification of objects and the permanent/temporal nature of the designated property.

Text units. The text, like any whole, consists of its constituent elements, certain units. There is a lot of debate in linguistics about which units make up a text or which units are considered text units when dividing a text into fragments. At first glance, it seems that defining text units is not such a difficult task. But in fact, this is not the case, and that is why there are many different views among students of text linguistics. For example, I. R. Galperin argues that a sentence cannot be a unit of text. In his opinion, the unity of the text can be a larger whole that combines several sentences, a larger whole than a phrase. A sentence, which is an integral part of a larger whole than a phrase, cannot be at the same time a unit of text.

Many linguists emphasize that the sentence is the main formative element of the text. In fact, it is difficult to imagine the content of the text, its relation to the objective world, that is, its correct understanding. Accordingly, the place of a sentence in a text system, especially its ability to generate a text, cannot be denied at all.

In linguistic literature, a sentence is treated as a complex syntactic unit, and a paragraph as a text unit. A sentence and a complex syntactic unit can be called the basic units of text, but a paragraph cannot be included in this single line. Because a paragraph is, first of all, a phenomenon unique to a written text.

Linguist A.N. Gvozdev puts a paragraph among punctuation marks. The paragraph serves as an indicator of a new direction of thought. The selection of several sentences or even one sentence in the form of a separate paragraph gives these sentences a certain weight, such a division is carried out by the author, depending on his purpose. I. R. Galperin, one of the largest researchers in text linguistics, also points out that the paragraph, like punctuation marks, serves to highlight the logical and emotional aspects of the text. at that, that this is a compositional-graphic technique. But paragraphs are an extremely necessary tool for writing, especially for a literary text. Paragraphs can be one word, one sentence, or multiple sentences. The organization of a paragraph is determined by writers quite arbitrarily, depending on their artistic intent. Paragraphs consisting of several sentences usually consist of 3 stages: 1st stage - the beginning of the message (initial, short message about the topic to be told in the paragraph), 2nd stage - the end of the message (the original message is completed, explained , is interpreted), and the 3rd stage is the output of the message (the message is completed, the result is stated). may consist of one sentence or several sentences. The organization of a paragraph is determined by writers quite arbitrarily, depending on their artistic intent. Paragraphs consisting of several sentences usually consist of 3 stages: 1st stage - the beginning of the message (initial, short message about the topic to be told in the paragraph), 2nd stage - the end of the message (the original message is completed, explained , is interpreted), and the 3rd stage is the output of the message (the message is completed, the result is stated). may consist of one sentence or several sentences. The organization of a paragraph is determined by writers quite arbitrarily, depending on their artistic intent. Paragraphs consisting of several sentences usually consist of 3 stages: 1st stage - the beginning of the message (initial, short message about the topic to be told in the paragraph), 2nd stage - the end of the message (the original message is completed, explained , is being interpreted), and the 3rd stage is the output of a message (the message is completed,

Integral parts of this whole are also the means of connecting the previous message with the next message in the paragraph (connecting means of connecting a paragraph with the previous or subsequent paragraph). The manual "Text Linguistics" says that the sentences that make up a paragraph are related to each other synsemantically (syntactically and lexico-semantically) and autosemantically (without grammatical connections, only semantically). Also, according to the structure of paragraphs, the following types are distinguished:

1) paragraphs with a phrase from a simple sentence;

2) paragraphs consisting of a compound sentence;

3) paragraphs consisting of a periodic speech form;

4) paragraphs consisting of a syntactic unit with a superphrase;

5) paragraphs with excerpts.

It may also include paragraphs consisting of mixed speech forms.

Based on the above considerations, a sentence and a complex syntactic unit can be considered text units, and a paragraph can be considered a subjective phenomenon, a compositional-graphic device that writers can use quite freely.

Text and its typological classification. The information transmission channel occupies a special place in the typology of texts. Accordingly, it is necessary to distinguish between oral text and written text type of texts. The amount of information provided in the process of communication is another basis for the typology of texts.[94].

Any text can be divided into minimum text and maximum text, depending on the amount of information expressed in it. In the text written in artistic style, the minimal text consists of poems dedicated to highlighting the topic, proverbs, sayings and aphorisms expressing folk wisdom, miniatures, comic pieces, names, poems and poetic fragments, usually consisting of several sentences covering a small theme.everything is clear. The inner side of the text is united by the integrity of the content, and the outer side - by links of various forms and syntactic means. For example: A writer without talent is like a chicken. It gives birth to eggs, like a walnut, and destroys the world with cackling (O'. Khoshimov). Or: What is love? Mankind has puzzled over this question since its inception, but cannot find an answer. If a person knew all the secrets of love, he would create his own model. Love is mysterious and eternal, because it does not fit into any framework (O'. Khoshimov).

We have included two passages that can be called the minimum text. The content of the first consists of two sentences. The content unification header is not provided. This task is assigned to the chicken and related words (chicken-egg-cluck). A writer without talent is compared to a chicken in the first sentence. The second sentence is given to fully explain or show the reason for this comparison. That is, a writer without talent was compared to a chicken, but what are the qualities and characteristics of a chicken? The position of the author is fully expressed in the second sentence. To ensure the integrity of the text, the words "chicken-egg-crack" serve as a semantic arrow. If we take the following small text, then the internal content of this text

---

[94] Yuldoshev M., Isakov Z., Heydarov Sh. Linguistic analysis of literary text. - Tashkent: National Library of Uzbekistan named after Alisher Navoi, 2010.

is revealed by a heading in the form of a question. The text consists of 4 sentences. Among the means to ensure integrity, refers to a consistent and complete tone, as well as the word love, which is a link, link and semantic axis of the text. So, the question is posed in the form of a question, and the answer is given through the text. I mean what is love? Love is a mysterious and eternal concept.

Some experts have put forward the idea that even one sentence can be equivalent to the concept of minimal text. Linguist N. Turniezov says that "a text can be expressed in one word, several words, several sentences, several paragraphs and several chapters." But the scientist also emphasizes that "it is inappropriate to study the problems of text linguistics on the basis of texts expressed in one word, complex or simple sentence. Because on the basis of such texts it is impossible to give a perfect description of the issues related to the translation of elements of the language system into speech. Linguist M. Khakimov also points out that one sentence can be equivalent to the concept of a text: "For example: Spring... Can this sentence be considered a small text? In our opinion, it can be considered a small text in the full sense. Because the phrase "Spring" uttered in one tone, contains a hidden meaning, such as "revival of nature", "everything becomes blue-blue", "the environment becomes beautiful." Therefore, a complete meaningful thought is expressed in a small text. But representations of this type cannot be called literally textual. Because the text is structurally a larger syntactic whole than a sentence. So, it consists of sentences. Meanings, called implicit content, are associated with the semantic structure of the word. It is correct to say that this sentence is a text only when it forms a single whole with the following explanatory or expanding sentences. If we draw conclusions on the basis of hidden content, then any word can be called a text. For example, if we take the word mother, such as "enlivening nature", "everything becomes blue-blue", "environment becomes beautiful". Therefore, a complete meaningful thought is expressed in a small text. But representations of this type cannot be called literally textual. Because the text is structurally a larger syntactic whole than a sentence. So, it consists of sentences. Meanings, called implicit content, are associated with the semantic structure of the word. It is correct to say that this sentence is a text only when it forms a single whole with the following explanatory or expanding sentences. If we draw conclusions on the basis of hidden content, then any word can be called a text. For example, if we take the word mother, such as "enlivening nature", "everything becomes blue-blue", "environment becomes beautiful". Therefore, a complete meaningful thought is expressed in a small text. But representations of this type cannot be called literally textual. Because the text is structurally a larger syntactic whole than a sentence. So, it consists of sentences. Meanings, called implicit content, are associated with the semantic structure of the word. It is correct to say that this sentence is a text only when it forms a single whole with the following explanatory or expanding sentences. If we draw conclusions on the basis of hidden content, then any word can be called a text. For example, if we take the word mother, Therefore, a complete meaningful thought is expressed in a small text. But representations of this type cannot be called literally textual. Because the text is structurally a larger syntactic whole than a sentence. So, it consists of sentences. Meanings, called implicit content, are associated with the semantic structure of the word. It is correct to say that this sentence is a text only when it forms a single whole with the following explanatory or expanding sentences. If we draw conclusions on the basis of hidden content, then any word can be called a text. For example, if we take the word mother, Therefore, a complete meaningful thought is expressed in a small text. But representations of this type cannot be called literally textual. Because the text is structurally a larger syntactic whole than a sentence. So, it consists of sentences. Meanings, called implicit content, are associated with the semantic structure of the word. It is correct to say that this sentence is a text only when it forms a single whole with the following explanatory or expanding sentences. If we draw conclusions on the basis of hidden content, then any word can be called a text. For example, if we take the word mother, it consists of sentences. Meanings, called implicit content, are associated with the semantic structure of the word. It is correct to say that this sentence is a text only when it forms a single whole with the following explanatory or expanding sentences. If we draw conclusions on the basis of hidden content, then any word can be called a text. For example, if we take the word mother, it consists of sentences. Meanings, called implicit content, are associated with the semantic structure of the word. It is correct to say that this sentence is a text only when it forms a single whole with the following explanatory or expanding sentences. If we draw conclusions on the basis of hidden content, then any word can be called a text. For example, if we take the word mother,

Maximum text it means a totality created by the need to cover a wide range of events. In the artistic style, large-scale works, such as stories, short stories, novels, epics, are as textual as possible. Ancillary parts, such as an epigraph, an introduction, and an epilogue, may also be included in such text. They serve as an additional explanation and commentary on the content and idea of the work, as well as on some issues related to the choice and coverage of the topic. The maximum text is externally designed differently. For example, if we look at the historical novel "Humayun and Akbar" by Pirimkul Kadyrov, then this work is divided into two independent parts. Both parts are named separately (Humayun. Akbar). Episodes are divided into 9-10 sections, and each section is named according to the place where the event takes place and who or what it is about (For example; 1. Agra. Hamida bonu arosatda., 2. Ganges. See , in). The total volume of the novel is 30 printed sheets.

Also in works on text linguistics, the term "microtext" is used to denote the complex syntactic integrity of a particular text, and the term "macrotext" is used to denote the full text. But the concepts of microtext and macrotext cannot be text types. Because they form a whole-part relationship. For example, A. Kahkhor's story "The Patient" as a whole is a macrotext (albeit a minimum text), complex syntactic units in it are a microtext.

When typing texts, their language structure should also be taken into account. Accordingly, one can distinguish between typologically stable structured texts (reference, document, annotation, patent, etc.) and freely structured texts (article, story, poem, novel, etc.).

Texts are grouped into different types depending on their content and the purpose of the expression. In this case, the main measure is the nature of the reported information and the purpose of its expression. From this point of view, in linguistics it is customary to divide texts into narrative, descriptive, debatable in accordance with the main forms of speech communication.

Another factor in determining text types is the basis of functional speech styles. According to the functional and methodological nature of the text, a scientific text (thesis, article, lecture, review), a literary text (prose, poetic works), an official text (certificate, resolution, order, description, recommendations), a popular text (article, colloquial, salutatory and speech texts) are divided into branches.

It is necessary to distinguish between two opposite types of texts, i.e., a literary text and a non-fictional text, based on which of the two important functions of language - communicative or aesthetic - takes the leading place in the purposefulness of the text. text. A text in which the communicative function is leading in its main purpose is better called a non-fiction text, and a text in which the aesthetic function is leading in its main purpose is a literary text. We do not always create new text during communication, conversation or writing. We use different types of text according to our needs. Sometimes we tell someone what has happened to us or what we have witnessed. We try to describe in detail a person or place that is unfamiliar to the listener. Sometimes we need to prove our point with various arguments, we feel the need to explain. Or recommend someone. We want him to be brought up on various life events or draw conclusions from what has been said. The purpose of communication is sometimes to convey a message to the listener. Sometimes we feel the need to ask for something. At the same time, we give recommendations on how to do something or order something not to be done. We use various directives, prohibitions, and exclamations to achieve our goal. The purpose and content of communication between people does not end there. A person wants to express his feelings, emotions, excitement, pain and sadness, thus influencing the listener or reader. In such cases, sometimes exaggeration We use visual aids such as similes and comparisons.

1) narrative text;
2) descriptive text;

3) explanatory text;

4) didactic text;

5) informative text;

6) interrogative text;

7) meaningful text of the command-request;

8) text with emotional expression.

Not forget? Fiction text may include some or all of the listed text types. It is also possible that the whole work was formed on the basis of only one of the types of text mentioned above.

QUESTIONS AND TASKS:

1. What is text?

2. What are the units of text?

3. What types of text are there?

4. What do you understand by fiction and popular science text?

5. What are the types of artistic text according to the author's intention?

LECTURE 2.

MEANS OF CONNECTING THE TEXT AND ITS PARTS. 2 hours.

Plan:

1. Proximity of content.
2. Content consistency.
3. Lexico-grammatical means of forming a literary text.

This topic presents thoughts on semantic proximity, semantic coherence, repetition, parcelling structures, nominal sentences, infinitive sentences, units of reference, units representing time and space, tense forms of participles, modal words, chiasmatic constructions.

Educational literature:

1. Abdurakhmanov Kh., Makhmudov N. Aesthetics of the word. - Tashkent: Teacher, 2002.

2. Boboev T., Boboeva Z. Visual arts. - Tashkent: TDPU, 2001.

3. Yuldoshev M., Isakov Z., Heydarov Sh. Linguistic analysis of a literary text. - Tashkent: Publishing House of the National Library of Uzbekistan. A. Navoi, 2010.

4. Yuldoshev M. Linguo-poetics of a literary text. - Tashkent: Science, 2008.

5. Yuldoshev M., Yadgarov K. Organization of practical classes on linguistic analysis of a literary text. - Tashkent: TDPU them. Nizomi, 2007.

6. Lapasov Yu. Artistic text and linguistic analysis. - Tashkent: Teacher, 1995.

7. Gilichev E. Linguistic analysis of the text. - Bukhara: Bukhara University, 2000.

In the text, sentences are connected to each other using various syntactic means of communication. They include various lexico-grammatical units, such as repeated sentences, pronouns, chiasmatic constructions, units representing time and space, participle tenses, modal words.

In our opinion, this type of syntactic connection is similar to the grammatical connection between the components of a compound sentence, only it appears in a more complex form. It is known that among the components of a compound sentence such meaningful relations are expressed as union, comparison, opposition, causation, condition-moment, definition, interpretation. These relations are three types of unions: syntactic means of communication that connect components in unions without unions, unions and subordinate clauses - intonation, unions, unions of words, sentence order, pronouns, repetition of certain words, second-order general sentences, temporary reservation relations, etc. P. implemented. It seems that a syntactic connection is established between predicates in compound sentences.

So, sentences in the text should be not only structural, but also meaningful. Consistency in content is just as important as consistency in the content of the text as a whole, for example: 1. The yard is as clean as butter. 2. Ahmed didn't come to class today? 3. You can climb from any depth to a height. 4. The task of the teacher should be to share dreams with students and teach them to dream.

Four sentences are presented in sequence above. But they don't have meaningful closeness. Therefore, it cannot be considered as a single text. In the following set of sentences, there is closeness of content, but no consistency of content: 1. The writer's words reach ten thousand or one hundred thousand readers at once. 2. Therefore, his verbal responsibility is a thousand times greater than that of others.

3. The word of a school teacher reaches thirty children. 4. The speaker's words reach thousands of listeners. 5. The words of the teacher Dorilfunu reach a hundred students. It is not difficult to see from these statements that the text is about the word and its responsibility. But for a correct, complete, and easy understanding of thought, the closedness of the content is sufficient. The integrity of the text is violated due to the violation of content consistency in this set of sentences. Now let's reprint these sentences: The word of the school teacher reaches thirty pieces. The words of teacher Dorilfunu reach hundreds of students. The speaker's words reach thousands of listeners. The words of a scribe can reach ten thousand or one hundred thousand readers at the same time. Therefore, his verbal responsibility is a thousand times greater than that of others (O`. Khoshimov).

What the author is trying to convey is actually presented in the last sentence. If the author had mentioned only the last sentence, the impact of this thought might not have been so strong. The writer completely and accurately achieved his goal, using the method of comparison and quantitative gradation: a teacher and thirty children in parallel, a teacher - one hundred students, a speaker - a thousand listeners, a writer - ten thousand, one hundred thousand readers. This is more pronounced against the background of gradually "expanding" lexical-semantic units in this text: 1. Institutions: school > dorilfunun > socio-creative school, v. 3. Number thirty > one hundred > thousand > ten thousand, one hundred thousand. The tone rises accordingly. The components of the text come into mutual contact and remote communication. Three or four days have passed. I gave the boy my phone. Did not call. One day,

In this text, we call the connection between the first and second, second and third, third and fourth sentences a contact (non-remote) connection, and the connection between the first and third, first and fourth sentences a distant (remote) connection. . The following lexical and grammatical means are of particular importance in connecting parts of a literary text:

1. Consolidation with repetitions. Text can be formed by reusing certain affixes, words, phrases or sentences used in the first sentence in subsequent components. Repetition technique is used to emphasize, confirm, express an idea in more detail. Increases the efficiency of speech. A chain connection formed with the help of lexical repetitions, pronouns and synonyms, a connection consisting of a set of components that begin or end with the same grammatical forms, is called a parallel connection. The following text repeats grammatically identical words, phrases and sentences, creating a parallel connection:

What happens when a mediocre person hates a mediocre one?

- Nothing will happen!

- What happens if the mediocre hates the talented?

- Nothing will happen!

- What happens when a talented person hates a mediocre one?

- Nothing will happen!

- What happens when a talented person hates a talented person?

- There will be a tragedy! (O'. Khoshimov).

There are several forms of repetition that also perform a stylistic function in the text: alliteration, assonance, anaphora, epiphora, etc. Alliteration is the repetition of consonant sounds for stylistic purposes. Assonance is the repetition of vowel sounds. Anaphora is the repetition of words or phrases at the beginning of lines of poetry. Epiphora refers to the repetition of words or additions at the end of verses. All this serves the compositional integrity of the text. First, we need to distinguish between variable and fixed repetitions depending on the composition of the repeating unit. This is a function that applies to all iterations. Repeats are divided into horizontal and vertical according to the place of application. Such repetitions, especially riy, create a unique melody in the texts. Also, depending on the category of the repeated unit, it is divided into the repetition of a noun, adjective repetition, pronoun repetition, verb repetition, etc. Phrase repetition and sentence repetition also differ in their syntactic nature. According to the location of these units and the distance between them, they are divided into contact (lack of distance, close location) and distant (distance, distant location) repetitions. Another form of repetition is called chiasma. Chiasm consists of two parts, the second part is opposite to the first part: According to the location of these units and the distance between them, they are divided into contact (lack of distance, close location) and distant (distance, distant location) repetitions. Another form of repetition is called chiasma. The chiasm has two parts, the second part is opposite to the first part: According to the location of these units and the distance between them, they are divided into contact (lack of distance, close location) and distant (distance, distant location) repetitions. Another form of repetition is called chiasma. The chiasm has two parts, the second part is opposite to the first part:

Long nights are so sad

Sad nights are so long...(I. Mirza).

In our classical literature, this kind of repetition is given attention as a special art. In the following example, each word of the first stanza is repeated unchanged in the second stanza. Beautiful composition, melodic and poetic:

Come to me, come to me, come to me

Your punishment is a disaster for me, and your hadeeth is a medicine for me.

Give me medicine, heal me from trouble

Your love is medicine for me and your marriage is medicine for me.(Babur).

2. You can also shape text and link its components using units that represent time and space. Events in a work of art occur on the basis of a certain time. Only the concept of time in a work of art differs from the regularity of time in real life. "Temporal lexemes serve to connect remote (non-distance, indirect) and contact (distance, indirect) parts of the text. Some temporary words perform the function of lexico-grammatical links and reflect the chronological order and sequence in the text.[95]. It rained in the morning. It was raining heavily. You loved the spring rain... Then the sun came out. Look the sun is shining

lying...(O'. Khoshimov). In the formation of this text there is a special service of time-semantic units. In the first sentence, the message about a natural phenomenon that occurred in this part of the day is expressed using the lexeme morning. The events described in the following sentences also happened consecutively at the same time. That is: in the morning > it was raining > it was raining heavily > the sun came out > it was shining. Text-forming means can also be lexemes denoting space. Typically, writers try to describe in detail the space in which the story takes place. If a lexeme with a spatial meaning is given, its description is also given. This is how text is created. Offers represent mutual contact and distance communication. The garden is very spacious, the paths are covered with golden sand, clear water flows from the marble channels.

3. Connection using parcel structures. In oral speech, in the text, there is sometimes a break in the whole sentence according to the need for communication. When the speaker informs the listener about an event, he tries to separate the most important thought from the others and emphasize it. It is known that selection is carried out in oral speech with the help of such means as tone, pause, logical stress, and in text parcel structures - text components.

manifested by a rearrangement according to the goal of expressive-stylistic. For example: 1. We must fight for freedom and justice. Or: 2. You have to fight. For freedom. For justice. The first sentence is a simple sentence in the usual way. The second sentence

---

[95] Yuldoshev M., Isakov Z., Heydarov Sh. Linguistic analysis of literary text. - Tashkent: National Library of Uzbekistan named after Alisher Navoi, 2010.

is a parcel structure. In this three-component device, the first part is the base part, and the rest are the parcel part. "The order in parcel structures is an effective word order with an emphasis on the essence and manifests itself as a grouping of parts of a sentence with a methodologically neutral structure in accordance with the communicative goal, a syntactic rearrangement. This is a reconstruction of the sentence structure (based on the syntactic isolation of its parts and contains a specific form of expressive expression and functional-semantic relationships). Brother Jalil was lying under the window (1). In bed (2). He is tall (3) Leaning on him and raising his head, he sees the garden (4). He improved the garden (5). (Sh. Kholmirzaev).

This passage consists of five sentences. 1st offer - basis, 2nd offer - parcel,

since the case of the base is not indicated, the premise is highlighted as a fragment, the 3rd sentence of the premise also served to emphasize the case of the base. It also made the connection between sentence 4 and sentence 1 more intense. That is, the hero lies under the window. He lies in bed. He lies on a high bed. If he leans against it, he will see the garden he cultivated. Sentence 5 is a parcel of sentence 4. That is, it served to determine the complement (connection) in the base (4).

4. Nominative (adjectives) and infinitive sentences are syntactic units that form the text. Adverbs confirm or indicate the existence of something. Pronominal sentences are not used in the text on their own, they are followed by other sentences or sentences that reveal and describe the content of the nominal sentence. The result is text. For example: Today is a holiday. The streets are crowded. Loud melodies are playing. Pass crowds of people. Cheerful, joyful noise shakes the spring sky (O'. Khoshimov).

Infinitive sentences are sentences consisting of one or more words, the grammatical basis of which is represented by the name of the action: Wait! A station where seconds turn into minutes and minutes into hours. Such words refer to an action and express surprise, joy, and similar situations and associated emotions in connection with that action.

5. Reference units and their possibilities of text formation. Reference units are widely used in our daily life, in speech activity, they actively serve the interaction, express the attitude of the speaker to the listener, carry various modal meanings. In classical art history, reference units are studied within the framework of exclamatory and complimentary art. Referential units are used in speech in order to attract the attention of the listener, to exclaim, to encourage. In such units, various communicative relations between the speaker and the listener are expressed. Examples; "My queen," he said angrily. - You are allowed! Take the most valuable thing for yourself from the royal treasury and go to your country! (O'. Khoshimov). Hey Ovsar! You don't know what to do! (S. Ahmad). Aisha, Aisha, mother Aisha, Nechun tears flow from your eyes. (A. Oripov). The reference unit "malikam" in the first example performs the function of a "springboard" for communication purposes, the referential unit "ovsar" in the second sentence performs a connotative function, openly expressing a personal attitude (discrimination, insult). between communicants. In the third sentence, the emotional reaction of the speaker is more pronounced through the repeated unit of appeal "Ayesha she." The repeated use of the impulse in one appeal serves to enhance the meaning and increase effectiveness. in which case, it is necessary to pay attention to the speech situation in which it is addressed. Factors such as the presence or absence in the speech process of the addressed person or object, the style of expression of the appeal, subjective attitude of the addressee to the addressee. The interlocutor can sometimes be a plant, animal or object. For example:

My dear, you do not have a piece of the mountain,

If mold is decomposed, a piece of stone will not come out of the ground.(M. Yusuf).

Or:

Buck deer, can I pet you

If I go crazy and go to the desert

You and I are strangers in this world

Buck deer, can I pet you?(M. Yusuf).

The analysis is required to determine the cause of such cases. With what purpose and artistic intention the writer or poet addresses, denotative-connotative meanings are considered in units of reference. In modern literary criticism, this method is studied under the term rhetorical appeal. In rhetorical appeals, as in rhetorical questions, an answer is not required, but "sharpens attention to the subject and causes a certain reaction in the reader." Basically, it is widely used "to express in poetic speech the intonation sought by the poet - solemnity, enthusiasm, anger, harshness, etc."

Questions and tasks:

1. What do you mean by content proximity and content consistency?

2. Give information about the repeated use of language units and chiasmatic constructions?

3. What are parcel structures?

4. What did you learn about the linguistic and poetic possibilities of pronouns and infinitive sentences?

5. What do you know about reference units and their linguistic and poetic possibilities?

6. What is the purpose of units representing time and space in a literary text?

used?

LECTURE 3.
PHONETIC CHARACTERISTICS OF THE TEXT. 2 hours.
Plan:

1. Phonographic means.
2. Alliteration, assonance.
3. Gemini.

This topic provides detailed definitions and examples based on terms such as phonographic means, writing more than one vowel, writing more than one consonant, graphon, alliteration, assonance, gemination.

Educational literature:

1. Abdurakhmanov Kh., Makhmudov N. Aesthetics of the word. - Tashkent: Teacher, 2002.

2. Boboev T., Boboeva Z. Visual arts. - Tashkent: TDPU, 2001.

3. Yuldoshev M., Isakov Z., Heydarov Sh. Linguistic analysis of a literary text. - T., 2010.

4. Yuldoshev M. Linguo-poetics of a literary text. - Tashkent: Science, 2008.

5. Yuldoshev M., Yadgarov K. Organization of practical classes on the topic "Linguistic analysis of a literary text." - Tashkent: TDPU, 2007.

6. Mamadzhanov A. Linguistics of the text. - Tashkent, 1999.

7. Sarimsakov B. Fundamentals and criteria of art. - Tashkent: 2004.

In the process of analyzing a literary text, it is necessary to pay special attention to the aesthetic properties of phonetic units. In a poetic text, the aesthetic possibilities of speech sounds are perceived quickly and easily. Because the poem has its own appealing tone. This melody is achieved through the methodical use of sounds. In poetry, phonetic techniques are mainly used, such as alliteration (repetition of consonants), assonance (repetition of vowels), gemination (layering of consonants). Vowel lengthening in prose expressiveness is provided by such phonetic techniques as layering consonants, repetition of sounds, changing the phonetic shell of words, raising or lowering the sound. The ability to "exactly" express the laws associated with the methodical use of sounds in writing is limited. However, the consistency of pronunciation and narration can be achieved with the help of phonographic means.

Expressing a state of mind in writing in works of art presents a unique challenge. Internal excitement in the psyche of the heroes, joy, sadness, approval, surprise, prayer, surprise, irony, pity, applause, questioning, stress, discontent, protest, desire, support. giving occasions such as support. For example:

1. Writing more than one vowel. This implies that the vowel is pronounced by lengthening it. The lengthening of the vowel clarifies the attitude of the character to reality. The scientific literature emphasizes that this technique is used to express that a sign is weaker or more than normal. For example, the weakness of the sign: "Dizziness" is said in a low voice so as not to be noticed... (P. Kadyrov). Redundancy of the symbol: A long white road, life goes one after another, row after row of buildings, if you think about it, my son, an interesting business of the world. (A. Mukhtar) "Turon" with the scene "Sharq" "four trumpets: g'oo-otu-uu g'ooo-ot! Go-go-go! Yes, your voice is silent, but stay without a master !! (A. Kadiri).

Also, the technique of writing multiple vowels in a literary text is used to express situations such as the surprise of a hero with something. For example: - Thank you. - His mangli tensed and continued: - Are you and I listening too? - O'-o'-o', okahan, you will pay in bundles. (Sh. Kholmirzaev) - Oh, it's you, look, I don't know you. You have come to our house again. Look at my absence. (S. Ahmad) I also hung my raincoat on the wall. - Oh! he said and went inside again. Tavakkal - Well... huh, Gulsara? This will be for one person! (Sh. Kholmirzaev).

It can be seen that this phonographic technique is used in a literary text for the purpose of calling, calling, attracting the attention of the listener. For example, calling: - I know myself, - he said, looking at the office of the collective farm on the other side of the ravine, descending behind the wooden engarak (forged gates): - Ho-oh, Boltabo-oh! (Sh. Kholmirzaev). Hasan recognized him. - Hey Ax! I say stop! he called out. "Axe!" he called with pain. (Sh. Kholmirzaev).

2. Writing more than one consonant. In fact, words that, according to the orthoepic norm, should be pronounced as one consonant, are pronounced intentionally in certain situations with the requirement of expressiveness and aesthetic purpose. Writers try to express this state by writing more than one consonant in a literary text in order to "accurately" convey the speaker's inner mood (tightness, joy, numbness, hesitation, bitterness, strong impact of the event) and the goal to the reader. At the same time, such values are expressed as the abnormality of the symptom, the duration or moment of action (occurrence at a time), repetition, high or low sound volume. For example, redundancy of signs; You are truly the best!

(from the newspaper), duration of action: - To be my wife, you don't know how to open vodka? - said the centurion, laughing. - learned! Look here! He slapped the bottom of the glass hard twice, the ball splashed out and hit the ceiling, then bounced off the floor and landed on a large glass on a tray, "bang!" ... it's over. - Ha-ha-ha! .. - said the centurion. I made your songs sound. Syntalok! (Graze). Oh, such a cow must have money in the market (S. Ahmad). After half an hour of bloody "gov-vvv, gvv-vv, ov-vvvv, ov-vvv" Mallakhon's horse was defeated and miraculously injured. (A. Kadiri). Moment of action: As soon as she saw Salim, Aunt Ziinat jumped up and disappeared from mind. Her high voice was heard, "Bummm," and the sky was covered with dust. He slapped the bottom of the glass hard twice, the ball splashed out and hit the ceiling, then bounced off the floor and landed on a large glass on a tray, "bang!" ... it's over. - Ha-ha-ha! .. - said the centurion. I made your songs sound. Syntalok! (Graze). Oh, such a cow must have money in the market (S. Ahmad). After half an hour of bloody "gov-vvv, gvv-vv, ov-vvvv, ov-vvv" Mallakhon's horse was defeated and miraculously injured. (A. Kadiri). Moment of action: As soon as she saw Salim, aunt Ziinat jumped up and disappeared from mind. Her high voice was heard, "Bummm," and the sky was covered with dust. He slapped the bottom of the glass hard twice, the ball splashed out and hit the ceiling, then bounced off the floor and landed on a large glass on a tray, "bang!" ... it's over. - Ha-ha-ha! .. - said the centurion. I made your songs sound. Syntalok! (Graze). Oh, such a cow must have money in the market (S. Ahmad). After half an hour of bloody "gov-vvv, gvv-vv, ov-vvvv, ov-vvv" Mallakhon's horse was defeated and miraculously injured. (A. Kadiri). Moment of action: As soon as she saw Salim, Aunt Ziinat jumped up and disappeared from sight. Her high voice was heard, "Bummm," and the sky was covered with dust. Syntalok! (Graze). Oh, such a cow must have money in the market (S. Ahmad). After half an hour of bloody "gov-vvv, gvv-vv, ov-vvvv, ov-vvv" Mallakhon's horse was defeated and miraculously injured. (A. Kadiri). Moment of action: As soon as she saw Salim, aunt Ziinat jumped up and disappeared from mind. Her high voice was heard, "Bummm," and the sky was covered with dust. Syntalok! (Graze). Oh, such a cow must have money in the market (S. Ahmad). After half an hour of bloody "gov-vvv, gvv-vv, ov-vvvv, ov-vvv" Mallakhon's horse was defeated and miraculously injured. (A. Kadiri). Moment of action: As soon as she saw Salim, aunt Ziinat jumped up and disappeared from mind. I heard her high voice: "Bummm".

Instant, drastic changes in the character's psyche are also given by writing more than one consonant: Well, what if you don't have to do it? That's all for now

you have reached... En-nasini... this world!(Sh. Kholmirzaev).

In the Russian and European philological tradition, there is a phenomenon known as gemination. In the Explanatory Dictionary of Linguistic Terms, this phenomenon is explained as "double consonant - the appearance of two identical consonants." In the textbook "Historical phonetics of the Uzbek language" this phenomenon is designated as "double consonant" or "double consonant". The conclusion is highly arbitrary. But this phenomenon is similar to phonetic changes in that it can occur only in a single consonant between two vowels, doubling occurs mainly in the sounds k, c, t, l, standing between two vowels, and only 2, 7, 8, 9, 30, 50 occur when naming numbers. can also be pronounced with a double consonant. The reasons for the duplication in the names of the numbers have not yet been identified. But the second t, l, k in such words as big, latte, yakka, yalla, chakki, ukki historically are morphological indicators, and there is an opinion that their doubling is the result of absorption (adaptation). Adkham Abdullayev used the term "folding consonants".[96]. By layering consonants, a complete description of the state of happiness and sadness in the hero's psyche is achieved in a work of art. For example, it will not be a lie if I boast that I took third place in Ayyarlyk (Oybek). You have no moral right to blame him, brother! - he said angrily (from the newspaper). The layering of consonants in the given examples served to express the subjective nature of the signs. That is, the satisfaction of the hero in the first sentence with his "work". The desire to emphasize that these are not "anoyi" is more clearly expressed by the folded consonant "h". The hero's anger in the second sentence is indicated by the twin "q". As we mentioned above, folding consonants is a special stylistic device. Since the sound that comes in cannot be folded, not all consonants that appear side by side in a word for various reasons have a linguo-poetic meaning. For example: - My sister, this kennoy (bride moon - ellipsis) is not cut with zigzags. From the first there are nine (present in spelling) children. The poor fellow thought that he would become a hostage. She gave birth to the ninth child, and in our language she became divorced (marriage + ha). (S. Ahmad).

3. Expression of incorrect pronunciation. In oral speech, for various reasons, there is a case of incorrect pronunciation of some words, mainly words of origin. Such a mistake may occur as a result of not knowing the correct spelling of the learned word, belonging to another nationality, not distinguishing between paronyms, not presenting the spelling of some words. This technique, called graphon, is used in a work of art in order to individualize the speech of the hero and bring the expression closer to oral-living speech. In

---

[96] Yuldoshev M., Isakov Z., Heydarov Sh. Linguistic analysis of a literary text. – Tashkent: National Library of Uzbekistan named after Alisher Navoi, 2010.

some places, the words are deliberately distorted and written in such a way as to cause laughter. For example: - I have to ask the secretary if I can come in. - Are you crazy, Nemat? - I am not Nemat for you, I am Comrade Babbaev, Comrade Khadzhaip (S. Akhmad). - Okay, that's right. His horse is Zulfikar, his last name is... - he looked at him, asking if he could say that (S. Ahmad). Borikhan was confused, like being in someone else's house. He did not know what to say to his brothers and sisters. That's right, he knew what to say. What if he doesn't know the language? thinking: "Salaam!" said. His liver was surprised, not knowing whether to laugh or cry. (S. Ahmad). "Your grateful father knew nothing but shepherd skills. I remember "Oshalo-ol!" those who came say ... - Not "Oshalal", but "Oshi Halal!" corrected by the music teacher (Sh. Kholmirzaev).

Alliteration. The role of alliteration in ensuring melodiousness and showiness of artistic speech is incomparable. Alliteration is the repeated use of the same consonants in poetry. This technique, based on the musicality of sounds, has been widely used in Eastern poetry since ancient times. Alliteration is referred to as "tavzi art" in the history of old art ("ilmi bade"). When we say alliteration, a well-known poem with the alliteration "ts" by the great poet Erkin Vakhidov comes to mind:

> *Add black, add pencil*
> *don't cry girl*
> *Ready to kill me*
> *Sword slayer look, girl.*
> *The caged bird suffers*
> *You don't put your wings on the ground.*
> *look at it*
> *May your sun warm my heart, girl.*

This technique can also be observed in the work of the poet Elbek:

If my chest is blue, then it's blue

If buried in blue, big-big,

If the lakes look blue and blue

Beautiful flowers to lift your spirits.

Alliteration is also seen in prose. In the following examples, you can see the alliteration formed by repeating the consonants b, g', q, sh, t, k: The entire page has become bij-bij. My whole face became wrinkled. I couldn't go anywhere - there were cracks and crevices. My face didn't turn into a face - it turned into rough earth. My face was not a face - it was a salt marsh! (T. Murad).

Sayings from children's folklore are also based on alliteration: A bunch of mulberries, a bunch of radishes under a mulberry. Mulberry pushes radish, radish crushes mulberry? White lid for white teapot, Blue lid for blue teapot.

We can observe that alliteration is also widely used in folk proverbs to ensure the integrity of intonation:

Don't fall in love with someone you don't love, don't lose someone you love.

The fox dreams of a chicken.

The chicken dreams of millet.

Satan plunges a stick into one who stands alone.

Assonance. Assonance is one of the phonetic techniques used to give intonational integrity, melodiousness and emotionally expressive artistic speech. The literature states that assonance is a melody formed by the repetition of the same or close vowels. The repetition of vowels is often observed in proverbs:

If you hunt, find out

Dol shoot at the target

Bread is blood, blood is life.

Even if you're out of your mind

Let the game be at home.

Assonance occurs as part of rhyming words, giving inspiration and inspiration to poetic speech.

gives a unique musicality:

I've lost my resolve in my soul

I do not know how to do it.

You came to visit us

Will you be faithful, my spring?!(A. Oripov).

Alliteration and assonance are especially important in poetic prose. The term saj is used in scientific literature to refer to two or more words in a rhyme or verse (sometimes both). Example: Alkissa, King Karakhan found out about the pain of his son from love, he was upset, his heart sank, his lower back bent, tears flowed from his eyes, he looked at his son and said a word while standing.

LECTURE 4.

LEXICO-SEMANTIC CHARACTERISTICS OF THE TEXT. 2 hours.

Plan:

1. Synonyms and similar words.
2. Paronymic and opposite words.
3. Words with multiple meanings.
4. Obsolete and new words.
5. Slang words, foreign and offensive words.
6. Stable compounds and agnonyms.

This topic provides explanations of such philological terms as synonymy, similarity of form, polysemy, anti-Semitism, antithesis, paronym, paronomasia, neologism, historicism, archaism, dialectism, vulgarism, barbarism, parems, agnonyms, agnomasia. Examples.

Educational literature:

1. Abdurakhmanov Kh., Makhmudov N. Aesthetics of the word. - Tashkent: Teacher, 2002.

2. Boboev T., Boboeva Z. Visual arts. - Tashkent: TDPU, 2001.

3. Yuldoshev M., Isakov Z., Heydarov Sh. Linguistic analysis of a literary text. - Tashkent: 2010.

4. Yuldoshev B. Fundamentals of phraseological methodology. - Samarkand, 1999.

5. Yuldoshev M. Linguo-poetics of a literary text. - Tashkent: Science, 2008.

6. Yuldoshev M., Yadgarov K. Organization of practical classes on linguistic analysis of a literary text. -Tashkent: TDPU im. Nizami, 2007.

7. Mamadzhanov A. Linguistics of the text. - Tashkent, 1999.

8. Makhmudov N. Honest and honest words. // Bulletin of literature and art of Uzbekistan, 1993. October 15. - No. 41-42.

In the process of linguistic analysis of a literary text, it is required to identify lexical units that show the writer's skill in using the language, emotionally expressive expressions are realized in a bubble, and reflect on the extent to which they served the writer's artistic and aesthetic goal. For this, synonyms, synonyms, antonyms, ambiguous, historical and archaic words, neoplasms, dialect words, foreign and vulgar words in the language of a work of art are distinguished, and what is relevant to the work, it is explained that it was imported. with the aim of.

Meaningful words. Synonyms are a unique means of showing the lexical richness of a language. A large number of synonyms in the language allows the language to more fully fulfill its aesthetic function. This is a phenomenon that has been understood, perceived and studied since ancient times. The Uzbek language is very rich in meaningful words. Writers try to find the most suitable images for the purpose among the significant words of our language and through them they try to express the psyche of the characters and the smallest aspects of the subject of the image. When analyzing synonyms in a literary text, it is necessary to pay attention to two aspects. One of them is that the author chooses the most appropriate content, expressed from two or more significant words.

In linguistics, there are three main types of semantics, namely:

1) lexical meaning;

2) phraseological meaning;

3) lexico-phraseological semantics.

Lexical semantics used for several purposes. To avoid the poverty and colorlessness of expression caused by the repetition of language units: The loud and cheerful voices of the two comrades, who spoke cheerfully and expressed their joy to each other, drowned out all other voices. (Graze). Pay attention to the object of the image: However, Islam is not in clothes, but in the heart, in the heart. (Graze). Clearly express the gradual growth of a positive sign: the other girls who came from Zebikhan are also nicer to each other, more open to each other, more cheerful than each other ... (Cholpon). To express the strengthening of the negative sign: Is the centurion himself as ugly and miserable as they say? (Graze).

Contextual (speech) meaning. One of the advantages of highly qualified writers in terms of artistic language is that they not only use ready-made meaningful words that exist in the language, but also use meaningless words in accordance with the needs of the artistic image in such a way that these words are also perceived in the text as synonyms. . For example: Just yesterday he cursed, cursed and said: "If I kill you!" Kissing, hugging and caressing his everyday life, they became "close friends" in the same breath. (Graze).

Phraseological meaning. The significance of phraseological expressions is widely used in the pictorial description of reality in order to vividly and fully embody it before the eyes of the reader. Impatience - fill the cup of patience, turn up your nose - inflate your nose, it's good to see - give your heart, put two legs in one boot - pull your legs, wave it into your mouth - An example of a phraseological unit is to bite wax. The semantic phrases that appear in the sentence serve to describe the quality, trait related to the hero, showing him in detail. For example: Isn't this the one who said that he won, won, and that his beloved came?

Lexico-phraseological semantics. As a lexical unit, phraseologism can have synonymous relations with words. For example: Happy - in the mouth, angry - angry, running - flood the world, etc. are considered lexico-phraseological synonyms. In a literary text, this type of semantics is used to exaggerate the situation and describe it in detail: As far as Kurvan-bibi was eloquent in words, so Razzak Sufi was quiet, silent, held his breath inside, was a stingy person.

Similar words. In our language there are words that have the same sound (pictorial in writing) and express different meanings. Such words are called homonyms. In linguistics, it is noted that there are three forms of homonymy: omolexeme, homograph and homophones.

Omolexeme when defining s, both uniformity in terms of pronunciation and uniformity in terms of literal (graphic) expression are taken into account. For example, pumpkin-I (human organ) - pumpkin-II (plant name).

Homograph's are literally the same, but have different pronunciations: volume-I (roof of the house) - volume-II (volume), atlas-I (a kind of silk fabric) - atlas-II (map).

Homophone's is considered equivalent in pronunciation: yot (< iodine) - yot, suthor (< sudhor) - milk eater.

Similarities are also observed in the expressions: raise on your head-I (revere) - raise on your head-II (rebel), raise your hand-I (vote, approve) - raise your hand-II (beat).

As a separate methodological tool, the work uses a melody created on the basis of words of the same type. In folklore, it is used to create laughter through askiya and payrs, and in poetry it is used to create tuyuk or words. For example: the poets Urfi in Kokand and

Kamal Khojandi in Khujand are friends with each other. Kamal Khojandi invited Urfi as a guest. While they were talking on the couch, Kamal Khojandi's little dog came up to the table and even touched the table, but he didn't say anything. Urfi was very upset and hardened and asked: - What did they call this mahsumcha? Kamal Khojandi: We gave one of Urfi's names.

Urfi: Let it be perfect!

Paronymic words. Paronyms are words whose phonetic structure is different, similar only in pronunciation and close. Abzal (originally afzor-tool, saddle-harness) - afzal (higher level of the word fasl), zahal (to be free) - holos (only), kush (good, pleasant) - quieter (a person's ability to feel, perceive). A stylistic figure based on paronyms is called paronomasia. In fiction, paronomasia is used for such purposes as expressiveness, melodiousness, creating a comic effect, creating a word. In fiction, such words (paronyms) are used to individualize the speech of characters, to show their spiritual and linguistic level. Paronyms are used for comic effect in the passage below. The hero finds himself in a funny situation, because he does not know the meaning of the words compote (juice, made from fruits) and compost (organic fertilizer fermented from waste): Walked and got out of the fight on the field of the fourth brigade. The head of the department was arguing about something with brother Ormon and brother Rakhimjon. As soon as he saw me, the head of the department said: "Comrade agronomist, I have a request for you." If Malal does not come, then it is Rakhimjon whose members do not understand compost. The head of the department was arguing about something with brother Ormon and brother Rakhimjon. As soon as he saw me, the head of the department said: "Comrade agronomist, I have a request for you." If Malal does not come, then it is Rakhimjon whose members do not understand compost. The head of the department was arguing about something with brother Ormon and brother Rakhimjon. As soon as he saw me, the head of the department said: "Comrade agronomist, I have a request for you." If Malal does not come, then it is Rakhimjon whose members do not understand compost.

"Thank you," I said, looking around, and plunged into the lecture:

- Comrades, compote is a very healthy drink, it is made mainly from fruits.

The more varied the fruit, the sweeter it is. In our Fergana region, compote is made from dried apricots, peaches and cherries.

So you didn't drink compote, you weren't born... I didn't have time to finish when people burst into laughter. (Kh. Tokhtabaev).

In paronamaze, a curious situation arose due to the hero's failure to distinguish between two similar words, that is, the confusion of the meanings of two separate words.

Opposite words. The presence in the language of words with the opposite meaning is one of the convenient means of ensuring the expressiveness, expressiveness and effectiveness of artistic speech. Oriental literature has made extensive use of this possibility of expression in language since ancient times. One of the arts that the poet really needs is tazad. This art is also called mutabaka, tibaq, tatbiq, muttazad, ittizad and takofu. In this art, experts say, words with opposite meanings are used. Abu Abdullah al-Khwarizmi, in his work "Mafatih al-ulum", dedicated to the study of the evolution of art history, explains the term mutabaka as follows: the word mutabaka comes from the verb tabaqa, which means "hind leg of a camel" "walked in the footsteps of its front leg". In the European philological tradition, this art is called "antithesis". In the works devoted to the language of a work of art, the terms of contrast and opposition are used. Concepts, signs, situations and images contradict the use of opposite words side by side. Usually, linguistic and contextual or colloquial antonyms are distinguished. For example: A new custom in an old village (proverb). Even though he was still quite tall, it was obvious that the end of his life was near. If so much land has been lost, then how many countries have been acquired in exchange for it, only God knows, and the beloved servant of God, black-eyed Miryakub knows! .. (Cholpon). Sometimes skillful writers contrast several words in one contextual synonymous row with several words in another contextual synonymous row at once in order to exaggerate the contrast in the psyche of the characters. For example: At this time, he laughed, opened up, rejoiced, blushed, looked at the sky ... Khadija Khan was crushed, burned, burned, humiliated and wept bitterly. (Graze).

Contextual antonyms are used in a work of art to increase the effectiveness of the image. For example: "Zelikhan woke up when he first heard about revenge from Elchin. If he walks and says that pain presses on his heart, like a rock, like a fist, then the volcano is gaining strength in this body ..." (T. Malik).

In this speech fragment, the words "fist" and "rock" entered into antonymous relations with the meanings "small" and "big". We can also observe a lot of contradictions in stable connections. In expressions: raise blue - hit the ground, have a bright face - have a dark face, have a white heart - have black inside, look hot in the eyes - look cold in the eyes. . Or a lexical and phraseological contradiction between a word and a phrase: greedy - an open palm, sad - like a mouth in your ear. In proverbs and sayings: respect the elder, honor the younger. Good horse, bad dog. The sky is far away - the earth is solid. In wise words: the one who learns what he does not know by asking is a scientist, and the one who does not ask is a tyrant. (Navoi).

Words with multiple meanings. When determining the skill of using the language, attention is paid to the extent to which he was able to provide the expressiveness of artistic speech. This can also be determined by the fact that he can use polysemantic words for a certain aesthetic purpose. Polysemantic words are a language tool that helps to expand the expressive possibilities of speech. For example: the word yuk is a polysemantic word in the Uzbek language. In the "Explanatory Dictionary of the Uzbek Language" the following meanings of this word are noted: 1) The weight that must be lifted and transported from one place to another; 2) Excess, causing a person to try and worry, anxiety, anxiety; 3) A child in the womb, a fetus; 4) Illness caused by insulting saints for religious reasons. Our honored writer Cholpon in the novel "Night and Day" managed to reveal the inner world of the characters more vividly and create a beautiful laugh based on mixing the 2nd and 4th meanings of this word in the speech of the characters: - I have a burden on my shoulder from ten to thirty feet ... - said the centurion. This, too, was said in a voice close to a scream. All three women could not understand what kind of burden it was. According to Hadichakhon, they made "Irim" for a thousand. Now there was nothing left but to "return" it. This idea is from other people's brains. This was also said in a voice close to a scream. All three women could not understand what kind of burden it was. According to Hadichakhon, they made "Irim" for a thousand. Now there was nothing left but to "return" it. This idea is from other people's brains. This was also said in a voice close to a scream. All three women could not understand what kind of burden it was. According to Hadichakhon, they made "Irim" for a thousand. Now there was nothing left but to "return" it. This idea is from someone else's brains

*It didn't work either... Only*Although Khadija Khan's opinion was firm, he did not see the need to hide it:

- It seems Ganim has plotted. Should I return it? He said.

"What your women know, don't tell me what you know, what you know, this is Azaim Khan..." said the centurion.

"Didn't you say "loaded" with your own mouth?"

Mingboshi laughed.

-*"**Load**What is the load if I say "clicked"? ask, bachagar! - He said.*

At this time, the people in the house gradually left and came to the middle. Thousandboshi continued:

- *Are you a burden to me?*

- *Why did we disturb you? Khadichakhon said.(Graze).*

The ambiguous word yuk is used in the speech of millenarians in the sense of "excessive care", that is, "three wives from ten pounds to thirty pounds", and wives are a sign of this word. 4th sense, thus a funny situation arose. We can also observe ambiguity in expressions. For example: the expression "come from the heart" can express joy and intense fear. As soon as he saw the girl's veil, the young man's heart jumped out of its sheath (Oybek). I can't say I'm not afraid, my son. At this time, the human heart will come out of its sheath. (A. Kahhor). Headline - come in for a while, get news; chat join people. As if falling from a roof - unexpectedly, from a cliff; in a rough way.

Outdated words. As society grows and changes, some concepts in the socio-economic, cultural and spiritual life are completely outdated and out of practice. When events of a certain period are described in a work of art, it is impossible not to refer to the ancient concepts related to this period. In linguistics, words expressing such concepts are generalized under the names "archaisms" and "historicisms". A linguistic unit that has a coloring of antiquity for the current period of the language is called archaism. Archaism lives side by side with a lexical unit representing the reality it names. Archaisms are used to realistically describe the reality of the period described in the literary text, to ensure the historical spirit of the work. ordu - army, khandasa - geometry, tilmoch - translator, mirza - secretary, When such words are used, like varnish - one hundred thousand, the spirit of the time is emphasized. Some archaic words have a stronger meaning than their modern counterparts. For example, if you pay attention to the archaic words "poor" and "poor", then the meaning of "have nothing" in the lexeme "poor" is much greater than in the lexeme "poor", because the composition of these words has historically developed. kam, which can be understood in the etymological analysis, it is felt that the same sign is at the "zero" level in the first. Archaic words are also used as a stylistic device to give characteristics to speech. In poetry, it is used to give an elevated spirit to speech: if you pay attention to the archaic words "poor". If you compare the words no-kam, which can be understood, in the first one it is felt that the same sign is at the "zero" level. Archaic words are also used as a stylistic device to give characteristics to speech. In poetry, it is used to give an elevated spirit to speech: if you pay attention to the archaic words "poor". If you compare the words no-kam, which can be understood, in the first one it is felt that the same sign is at the "zero" level. Archaic words are also used as a stylistic device to give characteristics to speech. In poetry, it is used to give speech an elevated spirit: Archaic words are also used as a stylistic device to give characteristics to speech. In poetry, it is used to give speech an elevated spirit: Archaic words are also used as a stylistic device to give characteristics to speech. In poetry, it is used to give an elevated spirit to speech:

At the hour when you knock the blue lid

The sun woke up in the blink of an eye.(G'. Ghulam).

Big on the outskirts of cities

Shosh, who found an eternal place.(A. Oripov).

Words that are not found in our time, but only denoting the names of historical things or events, are called historicisms (historical words). The difference between historicism and archaism is that today there is no other lexical unit representing this historical reality, therefore historicism is the only name for the phenomenon that it represents. For example; When words such as amin, bailiff, mingboshi, nayib, elikboshi, ponsad are used in a literary text, the reader recalls the historical reality associated with the public administration system. Historical words are also used in fiction to realistically describe the reality of the past.

When analyzing obsolete words in the language of a work of art, one cannot ignore the period in which the work was written. Because "words can become obsolete in the period when the writer lived and worked, and the work was in active use during the period when the work was written and then fell into disuse." he can.

New words. Leximes are neologisms or new words that have a color of novelty and are formed to express new things, events and concepts. A neologism may belong to the language as a whole or to the speech of an individual. The first is called a universal neologism, and the second is called an individual speech neologism. In a work of art, the neologisms of individual speech acquire artistic and aesthetic significance. Experienced writers try to express reality in a unique, original, and novel way. That's why they use new, strange words that aren't used yet or aren't used at all. This can be seen in the following examples: 1. I have a choice between these two nights! I am a demon, I am grass, I am fire. 2. Miryokub Akbarali despises, humiliates and laughs at his behavior. 3. I will come in the spring, I walked (Cholpon). 4. Bajarajak explains my work in detail. 5. I went to the herd to rest. (T. Murad). Our director comes out of the cabin. (T. Murad).

dialect words. Writers use dialect-specific words based on the need for images that are believable and alive, as in life, without detaching their characters from the area and environment in which they live. Dialect words, vividly reflecting the local flavor and territorial affiliation, "perform a certain aesthetic function in artistic speech. However, the aesthetic value of dialectisms is associated with their norm in artistic speech, with how they are used and what dialectisms are used in this case. In the literature on linguistics, it can be noted that dialect units are classified as phonetic, lexical and grammatical dialectisms.

phonetic dialectic, this is mainly manifested in the forms of changing sounds, increasing the sound, decreasing the sound and layering the sounds. For example: 1. Zebi's heart, compressed and rusty in winter, opened with the warm breath of spring; now, although he was in a cart covered with straw, he could already go to the fields (Cholpon). 2. The whole family of nannies massaged their breasts around the spread bag (Cholpon). 3. Have I had diarrhea? 4. There is a TV inside, my brother. 5. There is a reputation, but a reputation!

Lexical dialectic and in turn are studied in internal groups: purely lexical dialectics, ethnographic dialectics and semantic dialectics. For example: 1. The old woman plays, stroking the side of the frame, Anahon presses the chewing gum taken out of his mouth and makes a "sock" ... (Cholpon). 2. Your nephew brought linseed oil from the village. I'm afraid of it (T. Murad).

The names of the customs characteristic of the peoples living in the territory of distribution of a certain dialect are called ethnographic dialectisms. The reality of the image is provided by the following words: Before entering the door, he hands his wife a wedding nine: - Where is your daughter? he (Cholpon) asked. The word exists both in the literary language and in the dialect, and words that can be used in a dialect with a meaning that is not in the literary language are called semantic dialectics. For example: I don't invite my grandmother (mother) to visit without permission. (Cholpon).

Grammatical dialectic we can note the presence of internal groups, called morphological and syntactic. For example: How many times did Kurvanbibi repeat this truth in her heart. We know it's not the newlywed's fault. The characteristic of the dialect is also present in phrases and serves to emphasize the belonging of the heroes of a literary text to a certain region and place where events take place. I voted. I lost you.

Obscene and offensive words. In fiction, words and expressions of a foreign language are used to create a certain image. Of these foreign words that are not included in the vocabulary of the language and exist only in oral speech, in artistic speech they indicate the place where events take place, the speech situation and the nationality of those involved in it, and the nature of the characters is used for informational purposes. Such units are called barbarians. For example, in the following passage, the barbarities mentioned in the speech of a Tatar official named Fachullin served to fully reveal not only the nationality of the hero, but also his character: Ohu, intelligent Malay Shul. Out of this comes an equestrian communist. He left the party. To prove that he was not religious, he ate sausage. You have seen it with your own eyes. Only a patriotic communist can eat such a sausage. Bravo, bravo! (S. Ahmad).

In linguistics, in offensive words called vulgarisms, a number of expressions are very clearly visible, such as an extremely negative attitude, discrimination, neglect, insult. Such words live in speech not by their nominative meaning, but by their connotative meaning. Insults are used mainly in the speech of characters in works of art. In the process of linguistic analysis, it is necessary to group the vulgarisms introduced into a work of art according to whose speech (gender, estate, position, age, etc.) they are used, in what situations and for what reason they are used. , as well as to determine their lexical-semantic composition, dialect characteristics, etc. Examples: - Hey! Go to the garden and sit with the children!, Momo asked... Has your heart gone cold? Now the pasture is wide for you! You hit the fence in the garden shake it! (Sh. Kholmirzaev). - Silly! said the old woman. - Where have you gone? (S. Ahmad). - I'm sorry, what? Did you touch me? What does divorce say? (Graze). They say that the prey belongs to the cave, Batyr faction said. (T. Murad).

Stable connections. Language units, consisting of a stable connection of two or more words, ready for input into the speech process and available as a possibility in the memory of native speakers, are called stable connections. Phraseologisms, proverbs and wise sayings are stable compounds.

Phrases. The role and significance of phraseological expressions in the pictorial description of reality, in its vivid and complete embodiment before the eyes of the reader, are incomparable. Phrases represent a kind of figurative expression of the conclusions made by people on the basis of observing events in life, assessing acceptable and unacceptable actions in society, generalizing life experience. Writers are usually not satisfied with the selection of phrases in accordance with the purpose of the image. Perhaps the characters are changed and remade depending on their character, mental state, lifestyle. Thus, folk expressions are polished and saturated with new semantic subtleties. There are many ways to process folk sayings, give them a new color and tone, a new interpretation of meaning. This includes "discovering a new interpretation of the meaning underlying the common phrase, changing the lexical structure of the phrase and expanding its semantic-stylistic functions, such methods can be introduced, as an introduction to the phrase of new metaphorical and figurative meanings. Various methods of processing phraseological expressions were widely studied by B. Yuldoshev. The most common in literary texts are:

1. Replacing some words in a phrase: If you remain silent for another three days, you will become as weak as a mullah's bicycle. (S. Ahmad). We didn't even say that such and such a Mingboshi would attract our attention. Why are you silent? Did you stuff your mouth with cotton? Is there a fool in the world who would throw an ax at his own foot? (Cho'Ipon).

2. Expand the content of the phrase. A new word is added to the phrase. In our language there is an expression to put the jar. Cholpon expands it in the manner of a ravine with his twin: As if the commander took away and shamed everything in the eyes of the people! Abdisamat and Yadgor Goat, Umarali puchuchs love making a ravine with their twins!

3. Shorten the content of the phrase. The use of some words in the phrase is done with the requirement of economy of language. But writers use it for their artistic purposes. In our language there is an expression to wash and hit the armpit, and its meaning is interpreted as "lose sincerity, lose faith, lose attention" Cholpon in the novel "Day and Night" uses it abbreviated as follows: After that, if we allow such arbitrariness of the villagers, we will have to a short time to wash the hands of the village. The reduction in the shape of the yuvmok served not only for the compactness of the form, but also for changing the meaning. This phrase emphasizes that we will soon have to leave the village. It can be seen that the abbreviated version of the same phrase enriched the art of the text with new meanings, such as "leave", "separate", "run away".

When studying the expressions used in a work of art, determining the number (base) of phrases within the work and classifying them according to their characteristic features, their structural and semantic characteristics, checking their function in the text are the requirements of linguistic and poetic analysis. . This analysis also reveals the ability of the writer to use the linguistic units available as an opportunity.

Proverbs, sayings and wise words. Proverbs are small, concise, sharp, meaningful, figurative folk sayings that convey a grammatically complete thought. The ability to clearly and concisely express an idea in proverbs is very useful for ensuring the effectiveness of speech. Proverbs are also used to ensure nationalism and the veracity of a work of fiction. Proverbs are widely used to enrich the speech of characters and achieve emotional expressiveness. The word good is cream, the word bad is dough. You have a door - you have a cradle. Even if the sparrow is slaughtered, let the butcher slaughter it. Solomon died, the giants escaped. Hamal keldi - Figurative and integrally stable compounds such as amal keldi are proverbial. Matals are short concise folk phrases expressing educational, instructive meanings, grammatically in the form of a complete sentence, used only in their meaning - in the correct sense. For example: There can be no meat without bones, rice without cottage cheese. Doubt takes away faith. A flower without thorns is considered a matal. Proverbs are concise, meaningful, easy to use and short thoughts expressed by certain people or used in their works. Such words that can be introduced into speech are also called aphorisms. In linguistics, proverbs and wise words are also called "parems". There are many dictionaries dedicated to proverbs and aphorisms in the Uzbek language. When analyzing a work of art from a linguistic point of view, it is necessary to use such dictionaries effectively.

Agonyms. The term agonim comes from the Greek language and means unknown, incomprehensible, unknown. Words that are unknown, unfamiliar, incomprehensible or obscure to native speakers of a particular language are summarized under the name of agnonyms. Agnonyms are an anthropocentric rather than a lingocentric phenomenon. That is, it can be considered as a phenomenon associated with the linguistic ability of the language user. Experts believe that a certain lexical-phraseological unit must meet the following requirements in order to be accepted as an gnome:

1. If speakers of the same language are completely incomprehensible, then they exist at some level in consumption: jomish (jomish does not grow tall, goat and deer run), olatoganok (alato "although it's hard, but it won't be like ice."

2. Heard, but not fully understood by native speakers of the same language: qualification, bachelor, fauna, file, issue, embargo, rocking chair, etc.

3. If the speaker knows that a certain word refers to a certain area, thinks that "only the owners of a certain area know it", but cannot clearly say: histology, sistology, axiology, paralysis, Esperanto, ethnography, anemia such as.

4. If the speaker knows that a certain word is an object, but cannot say what it is: hantal, anguz, tuvok, koshin, caffeine, escort, etc.

5. If a native speaker knows the most general form of a word, but cannot name its private parts: Sakura, what kind of tree, where does it grow, what shape? An aquatic animal, but which one? Avocado is a fruit, but what kind of fruit? Also, even if a native speaker does not know or cannot explain the meaning of a certain word when it is used frequently and appropriately in the speech process, this unit is considered an agnome; such as spirituality, ankov, aqida, gaya, value, hamiyat, buyer.

В художественной литературе агнонимы выполняют особую эстетическую функцию. Агномазия – это явление использования агнонимов в художественном тексте с методологической целью. К числу возложенных на агномазию задач можно отнести такие, как отражение мировоззрения персонажей, индивидуализация их речи, выполнение иллюстративной функции. В приведенном ниже отрывке подчеркнутые агнономические единицы в основном употребляются в речи специалиста-фармацевта (лекция преподавателя) и носят иллюстративный характер. Для читателя значение этих слов не столь важно. У них есть информация только о роли героя: «Я сел в первом ряду и открыл свою лекционную тетрадь. Садир Фузейлович спокойно прошел и продолжил свою лекцию. - Снотворные вещества уменьшают возбудительные сеансы в нейронах, уменьшают возбуждающее влияние ретикулярной формации на кору головного мозга и тем самым вызывают сон. Я медленно повернулся и посмотрел. Музаффар тоже сидел, не сводя с меня глаз. Его борода выросла. Волосы не причесаны, рубашка помята... Он бы никогда так не ходил. Была поговорка.

- Among sleeping pills, the most effective drugs, - Sadir Fuzaylovich raised his voice, - are barbiturates. Among them, phenobarbital is currently the most powerful. This drug is taken as a sleeping pill, as well as convulsive, epilepto-convulsive medicine in the form of a powder or tablets in an amount of 0.1-0.2 grams. My mother also took phenobarbital yesterday. Two tablets. 0.2 grams! Then he fell asleep. I didn't hesitate. Last night I hated my moon for the first time."(O'. Khoshimov. "Between two doors"). In the following text, we can see that the comic effect was created because the elder did not know the meaning of the word bankrupt: A young businessman invited an elder from his neighborhood to his house. Looking at the young man, whose house will soon be filled with people, the father slowly asked:

- Yes, my child, the world?

- Peace, father, peace. I became a bit bankrupt. "Send him a blessing," said the businessman.

"Amen, please, go broke from now on," the father pleaded!

After allLet the father know about the bankruptcy!

In the work of Abdulla Kahkhor "Teacher of Literature", such gnomes as "Practicum", "Minimum", "Maximum", "Retention", "Standing", "Mering", "Dumping" served as an individualization of

Bakijon Bagaev's speech. So Bagijon Bagoev embodies before our eyes the image of people who use words that others (even himself) do not understand.

QUESTIONS AND TASKS:

1. What are the goals of using similar, similar and opposite words in a literary text?

2. How is the term mutabaqa explained in the work of Abu Abdullah al-Khwarizmi "Mafatih al-Ulum"?

3. For what purposes are neologisms, historicisms and archaisms used in literary texts?

4. For what purposes is dialectism, vulgarism and barbarism used in a literary text?

5. What are parems?

6. What is agnomism and agnomasia?

LECTURE 5
MORPHOLOGICAL CHARACTERISTICS OF THE ARTISTIC TEXT. 2 hours.

Plan:

1. The use of morphological units in a literary text.

2. Morphological parallelism.

3. Linguistic possibilities of categories and units of phrases.

This topic discusses morphological parallelism, affixal synonymy, affixal homonymy, affixal antonymy, anthroponymy, antonomasia, etc.

Educational literature:

1. Abdurakhmanov Kh., Makhmudov N. Aesthetics of the word. - Tashkent: Teacher, 2002.

2. Boboev T., Boboeva Z. Visual arts. - Tashkent: TDPU, 2001.

3. Yuldoshev M., Isakov Z., Heydarov Sh. Linguistic analysis of a literary text. - Tashkent: Publishing House of the National Library of Uzbekistan. A. Navoi, 2010.

4. Yuldoshev B. Fundamentals of phraseological methodology. - Samarkand, 1999.

5. Yuldoshev M. Linguo-poetics of a literary text. - Tashkent: Science, 2008.

6. Yuldoshev M., Yadgarov K. Organization of practical classes on linguistic analysis of a literary text. - Tashkent: TDPU them. Nizomi, 2007.

7. Mamadzhanov A. Linguistics of the text. - Tashkent, 1999.

8. Makhmudov N. Honest and honest words. // Newspaper "Literature and Art of Uzbekistan", 1993. October 15. - No. 41-42.

1. The use of morphological units in a literary text. When analyzing the linguistic features of a literary text, it is necessary to take into account cases associated with the use of morphological units. Expressiveness-emotionality is understood through special word forms, which are the aesthetic function of morphological units, as well as through the special use of word forms with a certain grammatical meaning and function. Expressiveness is clearly visible in words that have a positive and negative semantic edge. In the linguistic consideration of a literary text, it is necessary first of all to single out a connection with such a meaning and pay attention to which category it belongs to, in whose speech, for what purpose, by whom and in what situation it was used. Usually they caress-kiss, respect-respect, words expressing the meaning of elation, grandeur, solemnity - these are words with a positive semantic edge. For example: little girl, mare, orgilai, girgitton, my boy, my white, my plump, my lion, my wrestler, my sugar, my sweet.

Words with negative connotations include words expressing subjective attitudes such as disgust, arrogance, contempt, arrogance, mockery, hatred, anger, sarcasm, and rudeness. For example: pig, cocky, arrogant, insatiable, arrogant, bedavo, makor, muttaham, besonakai, satang, mugombir, shilkim. Identifying and evaluating the factors that create such meanings is the basis of linguistic analysis. The scope of research in poetic morphology is extremely wide, and one of them is the study of specific applied affixes. In the process of poetic research of affixes, first of all, their division into different lexical and grammatical categories is taken into account. In the Uzbek language, a diminutive form with suffixes -cha, -chak, -chak; The affectionate form is formed with the help of affixes -jon, -khan, -oy, -(a)lok. Respect, contempt, irony, meanings such as generalization and classification are formed with the -lar affix. The suffix -gina reveals the meanings of border, caress, proximity. In the process of analysis, not all morphological units used in the text are discussed, but morphological features in which the aesthetic purpose is clearly visible and the writer's artistic intention is expressed. For example, one of the most used means of artistic representation is repetition. The purpose of using morphological parallelism, a methodological tool resulting from the repetition of morphological units, can be studied linguistically. Morphological parallelism is a method of reusing words and grammatical means in a speech fragment that do not have an independent lexical meaning. In this case, the auxiliary words used in parallel within the framework of one syntactic device, the exact repetition of formative additions is assumed. Often there is a parallel use of morphological units with a special aesthetic purpose in poetic speech.

Motherland, I still have a soul
I am yours, I am yours
Even if I die, you are here
I am yours, I am yours.(E. Vakhidov).

Morphological (syntactic) parallelism in a prose text is often observed at the beginning of fairy tales. In the following example, the repetition of the stressed form of the imperfective verb has a unique melodiousness, musicality, and through this form of the verb a stable whole is formed with a sign of constancy: Dark, wolf - beaver, fox - artisan, crow - crow, sparrow - bird, turtle - scales, frog - watchman ... (from a fairy tale).

It will not be enough to note or emphasize the presence of morphological parallelism or any figurative and expressive device used in a work of art. The main purpose of this type of visual media or art is to what extent the writer wants to express; it should be focused on determining whether it serves free, convenient, attractive, or artistic expression. Otherwise, it becomes dull and boring. The tools of artistic representation are the tools that serve art by their name. This is not what we should strive for, and not the main goal.

Analysis of the poetic possibilities of plural categories, possessive, consonant categories and forms of subjective evaluation of a group of nouns is considered one of the important issues of linguopoetics. In the relevant literature, the use of this suffix to express respect, sarcasm, insult, uncertainty, amplification, repetition, emphasis is justified by specific examples. The ability of the plural suffix to fully reflect various emotions in the psyche of the characters is clearly visible in comparison with other suffixes.

"When the owner of the action or state expressed in the sentence is not a person, in the Turkic languages, including Uzbek, even if it is in the possessive form of the plural, the corresponding verb does not take a plural suffix, i.e. the leaves don't fall, but the leaves do. But Abdullah Kadiri also uses "-lar" in such places, he chooses such a style of depiction that -lar acquires a special subtle meaning. This is especially evident in the description relating to Kumush and Otabek: (…) on the other hand, the deft eyes that captured him seemed to be looking at him with hatred, as if shouting that he was unfaithful and unpromising.

A similar situation can be observed in the poems of Rauf Parfi:

The rain didn't stop for a long day

Frozen branches broke.

The rain didn't stop for a long day

The leaves have died.

The possessive form can also express modal meanings such as caress, lay down, mourn, appeasement, pity, sarcasm, sarcasm, pride, arrogance, modesty, in addition to the meaning of pure possession and ownership. In this example, the hero's spiritual world is revealed through the form of possession. The writer managed to accurately reflect the image of the hero, who is used to being proud of his disgusting deeds and treating the person in front of him in a tone of arrogance, self-conceit or humiliation: - The mind is not old, the mind is in the head, yes! - says General Skobelev. - I brought Khiva to its knees at the age of thirty! Here, at thirty-two, I snapped Kokan like millet! What did you get by defeating the Saxon? (T. Murad). It is also possible to make observations related to the use of proper names (anthroponyms) for a specific purpose. Because some names used in a work of art help to determine the artistic and aesthetic intent of the writer. The phenomenon associated with the use of nouns in such problems is summarized in some literature under the name antonomasia. In Uzbek literature, names that reveal character traits and cause meaningful laughter often appear in the comic works of Abdulla Kadiri, Abdulla Kahkhor, Said Ahmed and other writers. For example, Salimsok semiz, Curzon, Sonavoy, Sovinak, Magzhava kori, Burnash abziy, Kalvak mahzum, Tashpolot tajang (A. Kadiri); Jonfigon, Domla Cholk, Norin Cholpik, Nabigul, Semiz Nazarov, Orik Nazarov, Yovkosh Olloberganov (A. Kahkhor); The writer's sarcasm is clearly felt in the names of the heroes of the work, such as Goyipnazar Pinkhonov, Oldi Sottiev, Tidzhoratkhan (S. Ahmad). Our skillful writers try to create unique images, establishing a commonality between the life, fate and psyche of the hero and his name. This is, of course, the language skill of the writer, and by studying such cases, one can penetrate into the poetic world of the writer.

The adjective phrase is also of great importance as a poetic device. It is used to form the most common epithets in the language of fiction. Also, the artistic and aesthetic effect is created due to the synonymy in the verbal group of adjectives, forms that form the degree of quality, and adverbs that form adjectives.

Numbers are actually used to indicate a certain amount in a sentence. But we can also notice that it is used to emphasize the meanings of abstraction or excess. In this example, the number does not represent precision, but in some sense an abstraction:

The groan comes from the turkey,

Heartbreaking cry.

Look, the field is covered in blood

Mangu is a dream boy.(M. Yusuf).

The number "thousand" in the following passage does not mean a specific amount, but a prolonged excess of the norm:

My love for the world is like a flower.

Until the heart beats.

You will live forever, my verse -

A crow only enters a thousand.(M. Yusuf).

Pronouns also play a special role in ensuring the expressiveness of a literary text. Pronouns prevent confusion that can occur when repeating a word. The repetition of pronouns serves to shape the text along with giving speech a unique tone.

In the process of linguo-poetic analysis of a literary text, special attention should be paid to words belonging to the verb group. Because the expressive possibilities of words in this category are incredibly wide. It is advisable to study the features of the verb in terms of mood, person-number, indivisibility, ratio, tense and functional forms.

QUESTIONS AND TASKS:

1. For what purposes is morphological parallelism used in a literary text?

2. What is affixal synonymy and affixal homonymy?

3. What is affixal homonymy?

LECTURE 6

SYNTAXIC CHARACTERISTICS OF ARTISTIC TEXT. 2 hours.

Plan:

1. Forms of manifestation of expressiveness in a literary text.
2. Syntactic parallelism.
3. Emotionally-rhetorical interrogative sentences.
4. Inversion, ellipsis, skip.
5. Gradation and antithesis.
6. Differentiate and compare.

This topic explains such terms as syntactic parallelism, emotional sentence, rhetorical interrogative sentence, inversion, ellipsis, silence, gradation, antithesis, differentiation, comparison.

Educational literature:

1. Abdurakhmanov Kh., Makhmudov N. Aesthetics of the word. - Tashkent: Teacher, 2002.

2. Boboev T., Boboeva Z. Visual arts. - Tashkent: TDPU, 2001.

3. Yuldoshev M., Isakov Z., Heydarov Sh. Linguistic analysis of a literary text. - Tashkent: Publishing House of the National Library of Uzbekistan. A. Navoi, 2010.

4. Yuldoshev B. Fundamentals of phraseological methodology. - Samarkand, 1999.

5. Yuldoshev M. Linguo-poetics of a literary text. - Tashkent: Science, 2008.

6. Yuldoshev M., Yadgarov K. Organization of practical classes on linguistic analysis of a literary text. - Tashkent: TDPU them. Nizomi, 2007.

7. Mamadzhanov A. Linguistics of the text. - Tashkent, 1999.

The syntactic technique is widely used to ensure the effectiveness of artistic speech. The linguist Adkham Abdullayev, who deeply studied the forms of expressiveness, thought in terms of such stylistic figures as "syntactic gradation, syntactic synonymy, special use of conjunctions, antithesis, monologue, silence, inversion, repetition of sentences, rhetorical question", emphasizes that it serves for effective expression. The authors of the book "Linguistic Analysis of a Literary Text" state that there are the following recurring main forms of syntactic figures: "such as anaphora, epiphora, antithesis, gradation, ellipsis, alliteration, rhetorical question". These methodological tools can be found throughout the literature related to the topic. We restrict ourselves to the following ten cases:

1. Syntactic parallelism.
2. Emotional speech.
3. Rhetorical interrogative sentence.
4. Inversion.
5. Ellipsis.

6. Default.

7. Gradation.

8. Antithesis.

9. Differentiation.

10. Comparison.

Syntactic parallelism. Syntactically identical sentences are often used in literary text. In linguistics, such devices are studied under the term parallelism. Parallelism (Greek parallelos - going side by side) is the fact that parallel sentences have the same syntactic construction. For example: The kitchen is listening. The gate listens, the stable listens. He does not know where the sound comes from (T. Murad). The main task of parallel blocks is to explain the idea and, most importantly, to be able to completely convince the listener. They are one of the sources of enrichment of methodological tools and are the most productive and effective syntactic unit used in poetic speech. Identical sentences enrich the effectiveness of artistic speech, enhance the meaning and detail the thought, serve to expand the fund of information related to the image object. For example: Koshchi Kalondimak - Kalondimak took a step. Cybor is an arrogant hug. Kerma kosh - raised kerma kosh (T. Murad).

In this example, three different actions of the hero are expressed by sentences of the same form, that is, step - hug - feed. In the following example, the database is expanded with parallel clauses in one action: Tom went headlong. He walked calmly. He walked wisely. Or: Koschey took another step, crossing his arms over his chest. He took a step towards the Maghreb. He took a step towards Mashrek (T. Murad).

Emotional words. Emotional sentences are sentences that express the extreme happiness or sadness of the speaker, or the emotions of a character, an emotional reaction to events. Emotional sentences contain special positive and negative coloring words (such as face, octam, smile/smile, rude, smirk). Through these words, we can learn about such psychological processes as joy, fear, anger in the psyche of the hero, as well as the subjective attitude of the writer to the object of the image. Emotional sentences include words and phrases of a positive or negative color, exclamations expressing feelings (such as oh, wow, shorim, eh, attang, bye-bye-bye), impulses expressing attitudes, and they are part of speech, serve to expressiveness. : What a nice morning! You can breathe at your pleasure! If that's not so adorable, it's spring! How beautiful is our village! (From the newspaper). Sarvarov grumbled: - He was supposed to catch me in the second performance. When I first appeared, this old man was sitting holding his brain. (S. Ahmad). - Don't bite my tongue, cock! Didn't I tell you that in the fall you'd crawl under the table screaming... Well, you're still fourteen percent away from being a rooster. In the spring you didn't say a word to anyone. You hinted to me, don't complain! (A. Kahkhor). Oh, an amazing life, an amazing girl! .. Alas, poor thing! Gulsumbibi suddenly said. Salinity was given to the girl harder. (Oybek). that in the fall you will crawl under the table ... Well, you still have fourteen percent before the rooster. In the spring you didn't say a word to anyone. You hinted to me, don't complain! (A. Kahkhor). Oh, an amazing life, an amazing girl! .. Alas, poor thing! Gulsumbibi suddenly said. Salinity was given to the girl harder. (Oybek). that in the fall you will crawl under the table ... Well, you still have fourteen percent before the rooster. In the spring you didn't say a word to anyone. You hinted to me, don't complain! (A. Kahkhor). Oh, an amazing life, an amazing girl! .. Alas, poor thing!

Gulsumbibi suddenly said. Salinity was given to the girl harder. (Oybek).

A rhetorical question sentences are one of the methodological means that provide emotional and expressiveness of a literary text. Rhetorical interrogative sentences that do not require an answer from the listener are affirmative and negative. Often rhetorical question marks are not included in sentences, but are used to enhance expressiveness.

words come. They lend an uplifting spirit to the speech and serve to emphasize the statement with strong emotion. Such speech forms are very useful when the hero expresses surprise, joy, surprise, doubt and suspicion, anger and hatred. It is widely used in internal and external speech, monologue and dialogic speech. A beautiful example of a rhetorical question is the following poem by the honored poet Abdulla Oripov "To the people":

Where were you when Mashrab was hanged?
Where were you when the shepherd was shot?
Did you ask Kadiri?
Have you been a shield when trouble comes?
Judgments are read in your name,
History is woven into your name.
what are you What is your magical power?
Why do you go to shows so often?
In front of you I yearn for a sad thought,
When you become a nation, you are a crowd?!

Inversion refers to the phenomenon of changing the place of parts of a sentence or changing the arrangement of parts of a sentence for a particular purpose. Inversion is a characteristic of oral speech. In a literary text, this technique is used to bring the speech of characters closer to living speech, to individualize their language: What if your child is taken away from you! Can't you see, people work here! (A. Kahhor). - Throw that rock! my mother said. I was driving a cart in the middle of the street. - Do you know why I followed you? - you can leave it like that. (Sh. Kholmirzaev).

And in poetry, it is often used as an important tool that provides expressiveness, melody and impact:

This world is like a market

It's like a market, and that's the point.

I didn't even see the two of them.

Someone who says my mother is bad. (A. Oripov).

Ellipsis (young. discarding, discarding) refers to the phenomenon of discarding parts of speech for a specific purpose in the process of verbal communication. This reduction is carried out on the basis of the principle of language economy - language economy. For example: If this is the case with Avilaga... her sad voice also touched my soul. (Yu. Akram). Please stop... Look at this! (Sh. Kholmirzaev). What were you doing arguing with that bastard? (S. Ahmad). "We'll find it," I said. Talents will come to me, even if I do not have an editorial office, not to you (Sh. Kholmirzaev).

In the first and second examples, the word "thing" is highlighted with ellipsis, and in the third and fourth - the word "person". This is natural for live speech, and it was introduced into the literary text in order to ensure the same naturalness inherent in live speech. When considering the ellipsis in a literary text, it turns out which part of the sentence is an ellipsis and for what purpose it is observed. The ellipsis is very common in proverbs. As a result of the omission of words, brevity and expressiveness characteristic of the nature of the proverb arise:

The bear is the one who is separated, the wolf is the one who is separated.

You don't know your stupid uncle, you don't know your stupid uncle.

Default (or silence) refers to "the omission of a word or group of words at the end of a sentence". In the literature, it is treated as a form of ellipsis. We can observe that this technique is used in a literary text for the following purposes: 1. To express the discontinuity and incompleteness of the hero's speech for any reason: - This soil ... Akposha could not find the words. Cathy turns to look. (T. Murad). 2. Expressing the deliberate silence of the speaker in order to attract the attention of the listener: - The fact is ... As the Minister of Sweden, Mr. Falonchiev, said, this land is the most precious thing in the crown of Russia, yes, stop! (T. Murad). 3. When expressing what the hero thinks for a while: - Is he ... a big king or a big minister? (T. Murad). "My children..." he says. The white-haired man pursed his lips and thought. - My children... - he says, - I don't want to call you children. You are living a bigger life. (T. Murad).

Usually the hero's silence (maintenance of silence) is marked by many points. But we should not forget that not all sentences with multiple dots are examples of silence. Sometimes the author himself explains the silence of the hero and its reason. In such a situation, the expressive effect drops to an imperceptible level: the Sufi, who says no to everything his wife says, suddenly entered his mind without saying no this time. After a long silence Kurvanbibi now with a serious face: - Why are you silent? Say "OK! Big man, shame on you. He has a good wife and several daughters ... (Cholpon).

Gradation (lat. gradatio - stepped, stepped fortification). Methodical process of amplifying the meaning of one of the fragments of speech. In fiction, the gradation method is used to compare situations, feelings and experiences, to fully express the gamut of emotions. In the literature, gradation is classified differently according to its characteristics: in essence: ascending gradation and descending gradation; by way of expression: logical, emotional and quantitative gradation; according to the material of the expression: lexical gradation and syntactic gradation. I forgot about my regrets. I will not inherit. I'm not a bully either. But where is my seven-ore molten gate? Wonder of the world? Gold, iron, zinc, tin, steel, copper, silver gates? Bibikhan gate? Lost gates... Stolen gates... Gates broken into coins... (I.G'afurov).

In this example, initially personal qualities are described in stages. Further, in the form of adjectives associated with the gate, one can observe a descending gradation: wonderful gate - iron gate - sharp gate. It then follows who owns the gate, and the reason for the gate's disappearance is revealed: the gate is lost - (actually) stolen - (and) broken into coins.

Antithesis (antithesis - opposition, contradiction) refers to the phenomenon of opposition, contradiction to logically comparable thoughts, concepts, intuitions and symbols. To identify the conflicting nature of events in artistic speech, adverbs, contradictory conjunctions, words and phrases are mainly used. Linguistic analysis of a literary text requires determining what the author's intention is. The skill of the writer is more clearly seen in the material of the expression, selected for contrasting realities. For example: If you lose your bread, lose it, don't lose your name! (O'. Khoshimov). In this example, two unrelated concepts are contrasted - bread and a name. Why? Why does the writer oppose these two concepts? In fact, bread is life, an integral part of life. The man works and sweats to find a piece of bread to eat. But there are those in life who have tarnished their name and honor in order to find this piece of bread. Bread is needed, but the name is more important than this example. Indeed, he who has lost his bread can find it again, but what if he tarnishes his name and honor? It cannot be restored. "Bread" in this example can also be understood as "everything necessary for life, wealth." Or: Be deaf in the circle of fools. Be dumb in the circle of the wise... (O'. Khoshimov). In this example, the units ignorant - wise, deaf - mute are presented as material for expressing the antithesis. As a child, the world is wide and clothes are narrow. When you get old, clothes are wide, and the world is narrow... (O'. Khoshimov). Units causing conflict (childhood - old age, wide - narrow, wide world - narrow world, narrow clothes - wide clothes) had the form of a chiasmatic construction and served to exaggerate the contrast. In the phenomenon

Oxymoron *Greek* it is a word meaning "harsh but senseless". They are also called "random connections", "unusual connections", or "unusual connections" in some literature. Such combinations provide expressiveness of the image with their individuality, novelty, unusualness and grace: Quiet cry (M.Ali). Examples of oxymorons are such combinations as fiery ice, fiery river, dead hole, black light, naked consciousness, blinding mirage (R. Parfi), white night, wordless conversation. Such unusual combinations are interpreted as a form of antithesis. It is known that an oxymoron does not arise when any two words are combined. Such combinations are the product of the writer's artistic thinking. Therefore, unusual combinations cannot be attributed to illogicality. They must be approached as an aesthetic phenomenon, What force binds unrelated words? What is the possibility of expressing their combined artistic effect? What made the writer create such "unfortunate" combinations? You can get to the bottom of this event with questions like

Difference It is said to determine the differential sign of two things, events or situations. Differentiation is also based on comparison and contrast. According to the way of expression, two poles are compared, close to the antithesis, but logically opposite to the antithesis. In this case, one rejects or denies the other. In differentiation as a visual means, it is determined by what features the characters differ. The analogy is also based on comparison, but integral features are perceived in the analogy. Differentiation involves the definition of a fundamental difference that occurs when comparing. As in comparison, the elements of the expression of differentiation can be arranged as follows:

1. The subject of differentiation. 2. Difference coefficient. 3. The basis of differentiation. 4. Distinctive formal features. 5. Difference result. For example: "There is a room in the palace, which is lighter than the others, and the rooms are covered with felt. When it smells, a candle burns in this room, and when there are cheerful and cheerful people in other rooms, the owner of this room is another creation. A young man of heavy character, large build, a handsome and white face, beautiful, dark eyes, a proportional black forehead and just turned green. So this room was enough to attract attention in terms of the building and equipment, as well as the owner "(A. Kadiri. Days Past). There are silk and silk blankets, when there is a black light on the other side, a candle is burning in this room, and in other rooms people are carefree and cheerful, the owner of this room is another creature. A young man of heavy character, large build, a handsome and white face, beautiful, dark eyes, a proportional black forehead and just turned green. So this room was enough to attract

attention in terms of the building and equipment, as well as the owner "(A. Kadiri. Days Past). There are silk and silk blankets, when there is a black light on the other side, a candle is burning in this room, and in other rooms people are carefree and cheerful, the owner of this room is another creature. A young man of heavy character, large build, a handsome and white face, beautiful, dark eyes, a proportional black forehead and just turned green. So this room was enough to attract attention in terms of the building and equipment, as well as the owner "(A. Kadiri. Days Past). and in other rooms people are carefree and cheerful, the owner of this room is a different creature. A young man of heavy character, large build, a handsome and white face, beautiful, dark eyes, a proportional black forehead and just turned green. So this room was enough to attract attention in terms of the building and equipment, as well as the owner "(A. Kadiri. Days Past). and in other rooms people are carefree and cheerful, the owner of this room is a different creature. A young man of heavy character, large build, a handsome and white face, beautiful, dark eyes, a proportional black forehead and just turned green. So this room was enough to attract attention in terms of the building and equipment, as well as the owner "(A. Kadiri. Days Past).

As you can see, the passage compares the cell, the objects of the cell, and the owners of the cell. What features of the cell were revealed during the comparison? Alone in the palace

how many cells are there But in the image it is divided into two: a (one) cell and b (many) cells. The signs that distinguish a from b are initially given in general form: a - beautiful (b - not beautiful). Then, when sequentially counting the objects of the room, they show the difference between them: carpet - fabric; adrasa blanket - a gray blanket; candle - black light; After that, the difference between the owners of the room is listed: the owner has a heavy nature, a large physique, a beautiful and white face, a handsome, black-eyed, slender black forehead, and a young man who has just shaved his face. The owners of b cannot, of course, be described in this way. For this reason, all people in b are summed up under two signs: carefree, cheerful. According to the expression element of differentiation, the cell (a) is the subject of differentiation. Because the differentiated object is the cell. Cells (b) - differentiation coefficient that determines the uniqueness of a cell (a) in relation to other cells (b). We can take the word "vision" as the basis of differentiation. Because the beauty that is present in a is absent in b. This character emphasizes the difference between a and b. Formative signs of difference: the difference between them is further exaggerated by the conjunction "than others". The result of the distinction leads to the definition of the artistic intent of the writer. So why does the author make such a comparison? To what extent are these expressions related to the essence of a work of art? On the basis of such questions, the answer to the fifth element of differentiation is sought. It is easy to see that there is a three-stage series of differences in the quoted passage. Step 1: Cell. Step 2: cell supplies. Level 3 cell owners. Analyzing such situations in a work of art, we will be able to present the writer's syllogism with a complex construction of differentiation, logic of comparison and comparison. Comparison means "based on the similarity between two things or events, expressing the sign and essence of the other more fully, more concretely, more exaggerated through one of them." Comparisons are used as one of the oldest figurative means to decorate our speech, especially the language of fiction, to ensure clarity and imagery. In the literature, when expressing in the language of any relation of comparison, four elements are necessarily implied, namely: 1) the object of comparison: 2) the standard of comparison; 3) the basis of the analogy; 4) formal signs of similarity. For example: Alisher is as cunning as a fox. In this: Alisher is the subject of comparison; Fox is the standard of analogy; cunning is the basis of analogy; -day is a formal indicator of comparison. In her monograph on the linguo-poetics of Uzbek folk songs, M. Yakubbekova noted that another element of comparison is the "purpose of comparison". The standard of comparison determines the poetic value and aesthetic significance of the construction of comparison. The more original the benchmark, the more original the analog device. When considering the means of comparison in a literary text, it is necessary to classify them as traditional and private author's comparisons. In her monograph on the linguo-poetics of Uzbek folk songs, Yakubbekova noted that another element of comparison is the "purpose of comparison". The standard of comparison determines the poetic value and aesthetic significance of the construction of comparison. The more original the benchmark, the more original the analog device. When considering the means of comparison in a literary text, it is necessary to classify them as traditional and private author's comparisons. In her monograph on the linguo-poetics of Uzbek folk songs, Yakubbekova noted that another element of comparison is the "purpose of comparison". The standard of comparison determines the poetic value and aesthetic significance of the construction of comparison. The more original the benchmark, the more original the analog device. When considering the means of comparison in a literary text, it is necessary to classify them as traditional and private author's comparisons. The more original the benchmark, the more original the analog device. When considering the means of comparison in a literary text, it is necessary to classify them as traditional and private author's comparisons. The more original the benchmark, the more original the analog device. When considering the means of comparison in a literary text, it is necessary to classify them as traditional and private author's comparisons.

Traditional comparisons are comparisons that are often used in oral speech and therefore have lost their effectiveness. For example: cunning like a fox, hard like a rock, muzzle like the moon, eyes like eyes, meek like a sheep, known as the muzzle of a horse. In fact, it depends on the skill of the writer how to make such devices, which are judged as "unusual" because of their many repetitions, serve the purpose of imagery. Brand comparisons are comparisons created by the writer with the help of colloquial speech based on his own view, observation, artistic imagination, the power of analogy. In such comparisons, originality, imagery and expressiveness are always clearly expressed. The purpose of any analogy is the concretization of hard-to-imaginable concepts, the clarification of abstract concepts, things-phenomena, it should consist in putting the most subtle aspects of actions and situations before the eyes of the reader in beautiful colors. For example: There is no trace of a Sufi from Burungi, a Sufi who just lay down to sleep for a week. Its color is yellow-yellow, like a candle in a mosque... as if it had just recovered from an illness (Cholpon). In the given example, the faded, yellow color of a Sufi, a priest, is compared with a mosque candle. It should be noted that the writer chose an extremely suitable standard of comparison for the psyche of the hero, because the hero becomes full of endless pain, the candle is also a symbolic image of burning. the priest is compared to the candle of the mosque. It should be noted that the writer chose an extremely suitable standard of comparison for the psyche of the hero, because the hero becomes full of endless pain, the candle is also a symbolic image of burning. the priest is compared to the candle of the mosque. It should be noted that the writer chose an extremely suitable standard of comparison for the psyche of the hero, because the hero becomes full of endless pain, the candle is also a symbolic image of burning.

QUESTIONS AND TASKS:

1. What is syntactic parallelism?
2. What is emotional speech?
3. What is a rhetorical question?
4. What is inversion?
5. What is an ellipsis?
6. What is silence?
7. What is called gradation?
8. What is called the antithesis?
9. What is differentiation?
10. What is an analogy?

LECTURE 7
MIGRANTS AND THEIR SOCIOLINGUISTIC CHARACTERISTICS 2 hours.

Plan:

1. Metaphor.
2. Metonymy
3. Synecdoche.
4. Irony.
5. Paraphrase
6. Exaggeration, grotesque, reduction.

This section provides detailed information on linguistic and artistic terms such as metaphor, metonymy, synecdoche, irony, paraphrase, exaggeration, grotesque, minimization.

Educational literature:

1. Abdurakhmanov Kh., Makhmudov N. Aesthetics of the word. - Tashkent: Teacher, 2002.

2. Boboev T., Boboeva Z. Visual arts. - Tashkent: TDPU, 2001.

3. Yuldoshev M., Isakov Z., Heydarov Sh. Linguistic analysis of a literary text. - Tashkent: Publishing House of the National Library of Uzbekistan. A. Navoi, 2010.

4. Yuldoshev B. Fundamentals of phraseological methodology. - Samarkand, 1999.

5. Yuldoshev M. Linguo-poetics of a literary text. - Tashkent: Science, 2008.

6. Yuldoshev M., Yadgarov K. Organization of practical classes on linguistic analysis of a literary text. - Tashkent: TDPU them. Nizomi, 2007.

7. Mamadzhanov A. Linguistics of the text. - Tashkent, 1999.

8. Yuldoshev M. Secrets of the word "Cholpon". - Tashkent: Spirituality, 2002.

Translation is understood as "the transfer of a name, a sign of one thing to another, or the use of words in a general sense to increase the artistic value, expressiveness, expressiveness of a literary work." The processes of transferring the meaning of a word proceed in various forms, such issues as these processes and the events occurring as their results, the types of these events, their specific characteristics are studied in detail in Uzbek linguistics. . Migrations are studied under the term "paths" in almost all literature. In the manual "Linguistic Analysis of a Literary Text", translations are classified as follows:

1. Tropes based on the quantitative transfer of the meaning of the word: a) hyperbole; b) meiosis.

2. Tropes based on the qualitative transfer of the meaning of the word: a) metaphor; b) metonymy; c) irony. The rest of the figurative means are given as the appearance of these displacements: symbol, animation, epithet - apostrophe - metaphor; paraphrase, synecdoche, allegory, epithet - metonymy; antiphrase, sarcasm - irony; lithota is a manifestation of meiosis. In the linguistic and poetic analysis of a literary text, one should not forget that almost all figurative means called metaphors are based on the logical concept of comparison and comparison.

Metaphor. The transfer of meaning based on the similarity between things, phenomena and events is called a metaphor.

Metaphor is one of the most common ways of creating figurative meaning and is called "allegory" in our classical literature. Two types of metaphors should be distinguished: language metaphors and private author's metaphors. Linguistic metaphors are a phenomenon associated with the development of language. Since such metaphors mainly perform the function of calling, naming, they do not reflect the stylistic coloring, expressiveness, and, consequently, the subjective attitude to the subject of speech they represent. Only the range of meanings of a particular word is expanding and serves to designate new concepts. For example: the human eye is the eye of the ring, the hem of the shirt is the foot of the mountain. Private author's metaphors arise on the basis of the writer's aesthetic goal, i.e. naming beings by adding their subjective relation. They will be stylistically colorful and have the character of a picturesque depiction of reality. That is why in a literary text it serves for expressive, vivid expression of the feelings of the hero, clearly and concisely. Metaphors of self-authorship always have a connotative meaning.

Sociolinguistic Factors of Speech Specification of Language Capabilities. The system-structural approach, which studied linguistic possibilities on the principles of "language in itself", "language for itself", prepared a great ground for a conscious and reasonable consideration of speech reality.

Communicative-pragmatic analysis covers the participants of communication, information, situations and conditions of communication, language elements in general. These elements make up the communication system as a whole.

There are important and unimportant elements in the system. Important elements ensure the existence of the system and differ in this feature from non-essential elements. In the system-structural approach, system-forming, system-forming and system-neutral features of the system[97]The division of types also corresponds to a certain extent to the importance/insignificance of the elements.

The communication system is characterized by heterogeneity. Each of the heterogeneous elements reacts differently to the speech implementation of language capabilities, according to its "requirements", "desires" and "desires" and capabilities. At the same time, there are also relations of harmony and compatibility between them.

The member element is active in the communication system. The communicative intention of the participants plays a paramount role in the choice of language options. Also, "reconciliation" with other elements is determined by the high degree of flexibility and flexibility of the participating element, which differs from other elements. With a high level of selection in other elements, the non-interchangeability of the participating elements in the communication system is associated with their organizing and organizational nature. Irreplaceability itself creates a high level of flexibility. This "firstly, determines the content and means of the ongoing speech communication. The content of the dialogue is created as a result of the joint activity of communicants, the choice of language units and discourse corresponds to the purpose of this cooperation. Secondly, constitutes the world of objects in the human imagination in action, and the presence of these objects is the first and foremost requirement of communication based on gestures. Gesture-based communication is realized only when the "universe" of ideal objects of communicants is shared.[98]

---

[97]Solntsev V.M. Language as a system-structural formation. - M.: Nauka, 1971. (- 291 p.) - P. 46-47.
[98]Tarasov E.F. Problems of studying, describing and modeling speech communication. In: Linguistic pragmatics and communication with computers. M.: Nauka, 1989. (–S. 5-33.) – P.32.

The characteristics of communicants (age, gender, social position, status, etc.) play an important role in the fulfillment of the communicative tasks of language units. "The essence of communication is manifested only in the totality of objective and subjective facts. It is for this reason that the departments "speaking", "listening", "performing" and "understanding" are distinguished as important components of communication.[99] The personal qualities of communicators act as a catalyst in the choice of language units and setting them a specific communicative, emotionally expressive task. This factor is especially important when using language units in proper and figurative meanings and giving them occasional figurative meanings.

The subordination of participants to a pragmatic situation in the process of communication is one of the general and universal laws of communication. Speech etiquette and culture of communication serve as a subordinating factor. In accordance with this, the principles of modeling and normativity apply to the selection of language units, giving them occasional figurative meanings and using them. For example, it is known that such units as "order, warn, advise, prohibit, suggest" can take a place in a speech structure and serve to clarify its content. However, a boasting speech act like "I can't boast, I'm smarter than you" is much more unlikely. Perhaps the person performing this act has the right to boast. True, he is smarter than his interlocutor,[100] Communication etiquette consists not only in the use of language units, but also "regulates" the behavior of the speaker, preventing him from failing:

Dodho got angry and mocked Unsin:

---

[99]Safarov Sh. Pragmalinguistics. - B.66.
[100]Safarov Sh. Pragmalinguistics. - B.87.

"Obbo, the miller's daughter!" How many sheep will it cost? If I give you ten sheep, will you come with a knife? One hundred sheep, will you go if I give you half of my country?

Uncina playing with coins in bozvante:

"I don't need the state, I would go if the state needed it," he said. This speech shocked the dodho.

- What you need?

He didn't say a word. *Dodho's question could not remain unanswered. Therefore, if one of them commits a sin, they will all be beaten equally, Unsin urged:*

- And you answer!

- Are you speechless?!

After his friend, who was sitting next to him, nudged him two or three times with his elbow, Unsin raised his head, looked at the dodho, who looked at him as if he were unfortunate, bowed his head again, but answered boldly:

- If you answer... I will go to Ganjiravon... - he said.(A. Kahhor, Horror)

Ansan's every action in the text reveals his personality. This identity manifests itself as a combination of politeness, respect for the land, as well as spiritual and other human qualities, such as courage, simplicity and humility. These qualities are manifested in every expression of his speech.

In the above text, although the behavior of the communicator emphasizes the subordination of the communicative situation, in some expressions of his speech (*"Let him die, he's a bad man, just one sheep... At least something worthwhile!"*), in some of his actions (looks at the dodo, boldly answers) we see a certain degree of detachment from him. This is determined by the personal qualities of the communicator. If her femininity and femininity conditioned adaptability to the situation, then her human qualities, manifested in her desire for a man, are manifested in her submission to the situation.

In the communicative-pragmatic system, the element communicator (person) is characterized by the extreme complexity of its composition. Linguist V.V. Bogdanov identifies the following characteristics of the personality factor:

1) language abilities;
2) Nationality;
3) sociocultural position (such features as belonging to a certain social group, profession, position, education, place of residence, marital status);
4) biological and physiological indicators (gender, age, health status, presence/absence of physical defects);
5) mental-psychological type (temperament, pathological indicators);
6) change in mental state in relation to the situation (mood, temporary knowledge, goal, interest);
7) permanent tastes, interests and habits;
8) appearance (dress, behavior, behavior).[101]

Of course, the linguist can continue this list by indicating their internal components.

Those who have a "privilege" in terms of social status, status, age, gender, and those who have a negative or neutral attitude towards these characteristics differ from communicants. For example, equal and unequal communicators differ in age, position, social status, gender, or other characteristics. The rights to use language

---

[101] Bogdanov V.V. Speech communication: pragmatic and semantic aspects. - Leningrad: Publishing House of Leningrad State University, 1990. -89 p. - S.2829.

features are shared equally among peers, peers or "colleagues". In this case, both can be evaluated as implementation-neutral members of the language feature:

I got on the trolleybus. I sat down in an empty seat and started reading a book. I didn't understand the content of the lines when I read the book. My thoughts took me far. I didn't even pay attention to the girl sitting next to me. At some point, he burst out laughing.

"You don't even look at the man, Brother Erkin?"

I turned around in shock.

- Yes, Kholida... - I must have blushed from embarrassment, Kholida laughed merrily.

I smiled at the awkward situation and felt sorry for him. Nothing changed. Her childish twinkling eyes, as if always waiting for something, and thicker lips, which gave an expression similar to the simplicity and relaxation of her face, did not change. It was in Holi. It was Holida six months ago who sat with me at the same table - at the school table. It hasn't changed at all... I was just surprised that he called me "brother". When she was in school, she always called her: "Hey, boy, devil!" (O'. Khoshimov, "I will be a prisoner of dreams")

Gender differences decrease to a certain extent in relationships between equals, especially among classmates. This is determined by a number of factors, such as the fact that they are in a close relationship from an age when gender differences were not paid much attention to, and that this closeness lasted for many years. The pragmatic situation also plays a special role in this. But his role may not be able to change personal factors in certain situations. Notice the continuation of the text above:

We both stood side by side and were silent for a long time. Then Holida asked again, smiling as before:

- So, since you're going to be a journalist... Can I see it? Holida took the book in my hand. - Louis Aragon! Must be a good writer?

I silently nodded. As I was flipping through the book, my notebook fell out. He looked at me. Kuyuk's brows furrowed.

"Won't you be upset if I see this without permission?"

At first I said okay, then suddenly I grabbed his hands. Photo! After all, there is a photo of him in the notebook! (O'. Khoshimov, "I will be a prisoner of dreams")

A single word (I'm stuck) expresses the communicator's attitude towards the interlocutor and his behavior in accordance with it, but also weakens the influence of the pragmatic situation (in this case, the speech situation - being in a public place) on the interpersonal relationship factor. In a favorable pragmatic situation, intercommunicative gender characteristics (manners, respect, idioms) also weaken, and the boundaries of cultural norms "cross" in the use of language units:

- Think for yourself, mother, how will I say it, with what face will I say it?

"Do you have a face too, dishonest?" Come in, it's been a long time, tell me. That's all. Or you can't even say it? After all, their mother also gave birth!

"You will be a woman, sister.

If you don't tell me, I'll come and tell you. You humiliated my mother when she was alive, now...

The woman rushed to the hotel. Our master blocked his way.

- That's all. Be friendly with your guests. I'll take my mother to Tagob in Pocchanga's car. When the people of Tagob asked why you brought a dead body into the garden, one of our clan lost his mind. I

say I couldn't lift my head in Zarkoni. I will hold funerals and other ceremonies here, I say.

- Speak with your mouth, mom! I'll rip your jaw off.

"Talk about the work you can, it's a man's job." (S. Ahmad, "The Morning Remaining for Ages") The cultural level of the communicators, the level of communicative behavior, as internal elements of the participant's factor, accelerates the implementation of the communicative plan - gives impetus to the process of communication.

The absence of "borders" between the participants in communication ensures their free use of communication tools. Also, the unilateral absence of a "border", that is, the superiority of one of the communicants in terms of position and position, enhances the function of non-verbal means, and they act as verbal means - the implementation of language capabilities weakens, and this happens due to the strengthening of non-verbal means. We see a vivid expression of this situation in the following text:

"The doppelgänger fell off the roof. Walked around the pool. The pool stood upright on a platform. He returned his hands. He pushed his stomach forward. No, I'm going to push my belly forward. An empty stomach was left in front ... Katie went inside and disappeared. He's confused!

Koschi pointed his finger at the peasants.

- Stay like that! He said. The peasants gathered at the foot of the platform. Koschey tapped his finger on the platform.

- Sit down! He said.

The peasants were crushed. Chordana sat down.

Koschei stuck his wrist into his back. Belcars sighed. He pushed his stomach forward. Kathy went inside and disappeared.

– *But but! He said. - Tell me who am I? The peasants looked at each other. He nodded as if to say, "We know." He laughed through his mustache, as if telling a joke.*

"Whoever you are, let's call ourselves Batyr," he said.

The ventral bulges forward.

- *No! He said. "But you didn't find it!"*

The peasants turned away and laughed. The peasants laughed.

– *When was the collective farm formed? the assistant said. - When will you come to your senses? Guess who am I?*

The smile faded from the faces of the peasants. Barry thought. He couldn't stand the end.

– *Well, tell me?*

– *What if we were peasants walking in the field?*

– *You went into the fog, you say?*

Koschey put both hands on his chest. He puffed out his chest.

- *It's me? He said. - It's me! Tell me who am I?*

The peasants looked at each other.(T. Murad, "One cannot die in this world")

It is rather a marginal form of interaction between position and career. Because in this case, the separation of people of equal status, the increase in their rank and the fact that only he knew about it, and the peasants, who did not understand and did not know this, did not behave like subordinates, created a funny and sad situation. The pragmatic situation realized (by Batyr Koshchi) and unrealized (by the peasants) led to the fact that non-verbal means were not accepted into their function.

The physical qualities of the communicator also play an important role in the choice and use of language tools. Note:

"Zabarjad walks around the table and sits facing another person. He, too, kneels on the table and stares intently at his interlocutor.

– Do you regret it? It's over, my friend, don't think! I lost in this case, what do you care? But I don't regret it. I seem to be brighter again. It was my dream, here I am. It's been five years! No one else will see this threshold but you. My word Zabarzhad! Come on, okay? What if you talk after all! Eee! - Zabarjad slaps the table furiously, as if feeding a small child. Then he suddenly softens and smiles. -

– Honestly, you didn't expect? "Even if he is old - Do you believe that the girl is good? Well, who would believe - more than thirty, so far!.. Are you shameless? Raspberry Shame! When there is no husband to beat and no child to be ashamed of, one becomes more and more sensual, my friend! ... am I rude? he says, regretting his action. - I'm rude. "You, Zabar, were supposed to be born a boy, but something went wrong," said the father. Indeed, as a child, I would not have walked like that."(E. Azam, "Zabarjad")

This is an example of the subordination of the individual personality to the pragmatic situation. The fact that Zabarjad is a "boy" is manifested in his attitude towards everyone, but also causes a weakening of the pragmatic factor in the attitude of those around him:

Zabarjad descends the stairs. Passing through the second floor, someone makes a sound:

– Zabar, Zabar, will you work?

– Go fishing! - says Zabarjad turning away.

A bearded man peeks through a crack in a cool side door.

– Why don't you do it to me! I hugged you when you told me not to fall into the water.

– You don't have a fishing rod, Zakir, - Zabarjad said with an innocent smile, who was used to such cunning of his merchant neighbor.

– If you haven't seen my hook yet, hey girl! - says Zakir, turning into pampering. - Wow, look at that figure! Pants are tight, chest is shaking! I will die, wow! (E. Azam, "Zabarjad")

Of course, Zabarjad is the "culprit" of this abnormal situation in the dialogue. His non-compliance with the communicative etiquette characteristic of his gender creates the conditions for others to cross the line of norms in relation to him. Thanks to the communicative reason, the pragmatic situation acquires a new qualitative change.

So, in the process of communication, while the participants are subject to a pragmatic situation, pragmatic factors are influenced by personal factors depending on their personal qualities and attitudes. This is determined by such factors as the activity of communicators in the communication system, the high quality of its organization, the ability to organize other elements of communication around themselves in accordance with their goals.

The personal factor in the socio-pragmatic characterization of the derived meaning. Derived meanings of linguistic units with a nominative meaning are notable for their communicative and pragmatic characteristics in comparison with their basic meanings. Especially non-linguistic, figuratively derived meanings are distinguished by the superiority of this aspect. "The use of words individuality this is one of the factors that determine the unique style of the artist. When using a new word, the creator pursues certain goals. ...Excasional words are created according to speech needs, and the event is original to express give a chance. In this regard, occasional words are among the important lexical units that create the characteristics of poetic speech.[102]

The communicative intention of communicants in the implementation of speech meanings is enhanced by the effectiveness of expression and the priority of using non-verbal means. Accent as an artistic metaphor, especially in literary textsfThe use of occasional speech metaphors plays an important role in the realization of the intentional goal of the speaker. "Artistic metaphor is a figurative-expressive, expressive means. This is a technique that increases the expressiveness and figurativeness of artistic speech. Accordingly, artistic metaphor as a visual means plays an important role in the process of artistic speech.[103]

In a communication system, the intention of the communicator can be set at different levels. For example, the intention to simply give information, to receive information may take the form of providing information for the purpose of influencing, providing information for the purpose of obtaining information. In the second case, a person's linguistic activity is formed on the basis of a strongly formed and consciously controlled intention. The nature of communication can be divided into two according to the degree of cooperation with the intention to influence:

a) information based on firm intention;

b) information based on weak intent.

The use of figurative expressions and non-verbal means is more effective in speech designed to convey information based on weak intention.

An example of an informational text based on strong intent:

---

[102] Umurkulov B. Vocabulary of poetic speech. - Tashkent: Science, 1990. (-112 p.) - P.50.
[103] Umurkulov B. Vocabulary of poetic speech. - B.60.

Zainab ran into the house. His face was as pale as a corpse's. Otabek left Kumush and picked up the slurry from the ground:

- Drink, drink, drink!

Zainab bit her back... Otabek threw a cup at her... Zainab's clothes were covered in goo. Then Yusufbek Hadji appeared from the corridor.

- Go away, go away! Divorce, divorce!

Kumush's eyes lit up and closed again when he heard the word "talaq".

Hadji learned about the incident from a doctor, so the current scene of the tragedy did not surprise him.(A. Kadiri, "Past Days")

The reality in which a strong intention arises is associated with the speaker's mental state resulting from it, and the context of speech is subordinate to the pragmatic situation. A person falls under the influence of reality to such an extent that he cannot control himself. Cultural discourse once again demonstrates its artificiality. After all, Otabek, the hero of the play, was brought up in a cultural spirit, and he should not speak in vain in front of many people (including women). But when the situation is tense and unstable, anyone can forget their identity. Helplessness causes anger in a person:*My people, it's been a long time, you haven't seen enough / You've cooked food you didn't like. You wore it for someone, / You didn't wear it yourself, / You discovered a star and made a name for yourself - people! / I don't have the habit of regretting the past, / A soul touched by mourning in vain / But I can't stop throwing stones / Time who expelled the furkat./ Forgive me, ordinary people,/ Remember you. Any terrible fate will come./ How many times have passed between you,/ How many Alishers have contracted malaria!*(A. Oripov, "Face to Face")

Of course, this quote is about attitudes towards social problems. But a personal attitude to personal, family problems takes shape. Otabek's personal life collapsed. For him, this world has turned into darkness. Bamisoli the sky fell on his head. In this case, a person is doomed to lose himself. In this situation, it is inevitable for him to use the word jalab, which he has never used in his life.

*Attractive*the basic meaning of the word is known. But Zainab lacks a denotative feature, which is associated with the original meaning of the word. And Zainab's act is even worse and more shameful. An extremely changeable situation and strong mental stress only increase the element of influence in the speaker's intention. The information component is weakening because of this.

The basis of affective intention is the desire to get away from the affect that causes suffering. This desire happens subconsciously. Getting on the bait and spreading the poison is the result of the speaker's desire to get out of the trap, which he unconsciously sets. This leads to the use of words in inappropriate figurative meanings. The state of mind destroys the mental control over speech.

An example of informational text based on weak intent:

Our grandfather's eyes brightened up. Tagin Sayrak turned and looked at the hill.

Two blacks remained on a rare hill. One fell in love, the other became a lover.

The lover and the beloved have become one and the same...

Our grandfather smiles.

- Here are our children! - They said. - Grandfather Khizr, bless your life!

My face is full of youth from our grandfather's smiling cheeks.

After the death of our mother, the tears seemed to dry up. Where did you sleep, young people?

Our hard-working youth applies it on the lips and on the chin.

Our grandfather wiped away his tears with his hands. They kept their eyes on the hill.

- Here are our grandchildren! - They said. - Service, my grandfather Khizr, service!

Our grandfather poured out something from his heart every now and then.

This flood can be called sadness or happiness.

Our grandfather's heart was filled with sad happiness. (T. Murad, "People Walking on the Moon")

Momos passed. The last seconds of our grandfather's life. He is alone. He is talking to himself. Moderate communicative speech situation. External and internal factors created a free environment for a person to manifest his natural or "artificial" (cultural) image. Speech intention is directed inward - to the speaker himself. It has no element of information, no influence. Speech has no purpose other than to relax. This goal - relaxation is controlled not by consciousness, but by subconscious mechanisms. Therefore, among the language expressions used, there are few figurative and colorful means that enhance the effect.

In a literary text, the author uses figurative expressions well to effectively convey his subjective intention:

Near the horizon / Beyond the blue sea / There is land. There is life in him / His chest is bruised, his chest is bloody. / The dark night loosens his hair / In this ruined land / A tyrant named Sultan / He oppresses the people.. (E. Vakhidov, "Fountain of Dreams")

According to the interpretation of the linguist B. Umurkulov, "the words blue and black, which show signs of an object in this poetic passage, are words characteristic of a neutral style. The combination of the blue sea does not evoke emotions in a person (the meanings of these words are familiar, it is of a socialized nature - G.N.), because this combination creates an image of the color of sea water in a person (it is mainly used in a person to create new information - G.N. .) By combining the dark night, the poet described the miserable life of people across the sea, "a wound in the chest, blood in the heart" and achieved an impressive image. The dark night is used figuratively, meaning "misfortune, injustice, destruction."nbrings its colors to our imagination.[104]If we say that the poet was talking about a veil blocking the view of being through the expression of the blue sea, then the expression of the blue sea also created a poetic image with the meaning of an occasional derivative. Listening to this inner meaning, one understands the harmony of the organs of information and influence.

The social meaning of anthropomorphic metaphors.

Metaphorical expressions in the poem "Valley of Happiness" by H. Olimjon, a famous poet of his time, are studied in detail. But today there is a need to identify the poetic value of pragmatically effective elements in a poem - the need to study the nature of anthropomorphic metaphors:

To the waters of the spring / He washed his face, He bathed in the bosom of the marble air / In the dells of Zilal / He stretched out his wide arms, With love of independence / **burned down** *the fields are blue.*

---

[104]Umurkulov B. Vocabulary of poetic speech. - B.68.

In lexical expressions with a separate derivative meaning, the inner feelings and pride of the lyrical hero are expressed, as well as the harmony and commonality of maximum impact with the task of providing minimal information.

The communicative features of artistic, especially poetic texts are characterized by which of the elements of information and influence has a higher priority than the communicative features of other, say, scientific and official texts. In poetic texts, the function of providing information is somewhat weakened. Instead, the task of influence is strengthened. Therefore, many artistic concepts and techniques are used in poetic texts, and among them, those based on figurative meaning are especially fruitful. Symbols and metaphors are effectively used in poetic texts. This is also connected with the expression of thought in figurative images, cases of the desire to exaggerate the inner content under the external meanings. Based on this, in all poetic texts with internal content, most of the words and phrases phrases are used in figurative meanings. For example, the famous Kazakh poet M. Shokhanov "12-3=?" The author's communicative intent of the epic is based on the apparent content of the poem.Gnot lost. "... It shows the bitter truth of the period of stagnation ... Yevgeny Yevtushenko once translated it into Russian. I wrote a preface for him and recommended it for publication in the Smena magazine. It seems that the magazine's staff noticed the meaning hidden under majos and did not publish the work.[105]

The communicative intention of the poet was to artistically describe the sad situation of the stagnant years. It is known that "Brezhnev did this on purpose to hide the fact that the rest of the

---

[105] Aitmatov Ch., Shokhanov M. The lament of the hunter who remained on the top (Apology uttered in the poem of the century) // Translation: N. Baki, Y. Khodjamberdi; Translation editor: T. Adashboev /. - Tashkent: Shark NMAK, 1998. (-432 p.) - B. 221222.

party members left in his condition, but the Politburo at that time was full of old people." In 1979, their average age was 70. For some of them, going down to the pulpit was a torment. In an anecdote common at that time among the people, someone in the voice of Brezhnev says: "I ask you to raise the members of the Politburo." The leaders of the Union republics, imitating the Kremlin in everything, did not lag behind the old people on Red Square in terms of age.

I wrote a little epic called those years. "The problem of grandfathers sitting in the Kremlin is a real concern."[106] It can be seen from the text that the goal of the poet is not to give information about the existing reality, because this situation is known among the people, everyone knew it. The communicative intention of the poet is only to express his "concern" caused by the current situation. But the pragmatic situation does not allow to declare it openly. As a result, the poet turns to metaphor. On the basis of metaphor, he also increases the effectiveness of his communicative design. While reading the poem, one can observe a number of language units that have acquired a figurative meaning in it.

The text also shows the second, that is, the general communicative intention of the poet. If reality were not surrounded by symbols and presented in a poetic way, then with such a description of reality, the conclusion about reality could give the impression that it is a specific case. But the goal of giving thought a methodological tone required the creation of an epic in such a state. The desire to show generality in a particular case is realized.

Therefore, any text with figurative content is created for a speech communicative purpose, has a pragmatic character and has acquired a general methodological significance.

---

[106] Aitmatov Ch., Shokhanov M. The lament of the hunter who remained on the top (Apologies spoken in Asra's poem) - B. 216217.

When expressing a communicative intention with sarcastic images and thoughts, the ratio of external and internal types of meaning is of particular importance when transmitting information with pragmatic factors.

Sarcasm forms a thematic group with such phenomena as cutting and pitching. However, among them, irony is distinguished by its logical value, scope, cultural essence. It is characterized by the fact that it is a product of a high intellectual and cognitive process, and its functional "stone" is restrained.

The organizing function of irony is clearly visible in its function of linking the text. Therefore, its intertextuality is combined with the principles of intellectual coherence and coherence. This sign of irony shows that this is a gradual process, a link between the past and the present, in a certain sense a historical phenomenon.

Of course, irony as a product of human thinking manifests itself at different levels and in different forms. In particular, his expression of the subjective attitude to being is associated with the intellectual potential and energy memory of the subject. Therefore, the role of irony in written literature, its place in puns as a means of imparting artistry, is of particular importance. Irony, as a unique phenomenon, manifested as a combination of artistic intent and thinking, has always been the fruit of folk wisdom, the product of the ingenuity of great thinkers. After all, the fact that not only separate artistic fragments, but also entire texts, even large works, are built on the basis of irony is proof of our opinion. In Uzbek literature, there are folk tales, matals, large canvases with the contents of a cup under a cup, such as "Zarbulmasal", Such works as "Don Quixote", which made a great contribution to the development of Western literature, are high examples of the art of irony. In modern Uzbek literature, one can find many works of art that are excellent examples of irony.

Fundamental socio-political changes and updates in the development of human society, first of all, are reflected in fiction, so a self-confident public is always more prone to ironic expressions. Of course, a person's desire to recognize this as a law increases. For example, the struggle between the old and the new is activated by irony as a supposedly "compromising" expression of their irreconcilable conflict. In itself, this "compromise" is a cultural intolerance, a rebellion at a high level, expressed through human thought. The proof of our opinion is that irony underlies the genre of satire and humor, which was widely developed at the beginning of the last century.Iis Abdullah Qadiri's "Feletons", created as a result of a cultural "compromise", were built on the basis of irony, which served as a great satirical weapon, and the writer's communicative and aesthetic intentions were highly harmonized.

The fact that the improvement, complication and confusion of international relations is an inevitable process in the world community requires an increase in the role of the media covering them. In particular, the formation and development of the information style in its own way, the complication of international relations and communication in political relations require the improvement and improvement of the journalistic style, which is under its influence and influences it. Therefore, today in political journalism, irony, intertextuality and other language games show new aspects and become a unique phenomenon separately takes on a social dimension.

Irony is a phenomenon or method based on the contradictory relationship between form and content. When the speaker observes existence, his and someone else's apparent relation to it requires him to construct the expression of the observed object differently, indirectly, against the essence. Although it appears that what is observed is different and unreservedly corresponds to what is being said, the speaker is pointing out the incompatibility of thought and expression for non-linguistic or pragmatic reasons. This, on the other hand, is associated with a false desire to "try" to take the funny for the serious, creating suspicious elation and skepticism.

Although he himself did not use this term and did not clearly express his life and philosophical attitude towards it, the term "Socratic irony" is popular in the scientific community. The essence of this term is perceived on the basis of the existence of a conflict between what is seen, what is seen and what is real. In many sources it is noted that it manifests itself in the following. The irony manifests itself, first of all, in the fact that Socrates falsely praises and applauds his interlocutors (the contrast between the initial situation and the expression of Socrates (and not his opinion). none of the interlocutors had the Socratic dignity and honor.In fact, self-abasement is also incompatible with its original purpose, between reality and expression conflict available.

Thirdly, the irony of Socrates is that the pretense of ignorance is actually a consequence of the desire for true knowledge and wisdom. Because, as Socrates himself pointed out, he knows that he knows nothing, and others do not even know it. He taught his interlocutors to understand the truth on the basis of irony, sought from them the ability to critically evaluate their own behavior so that a person could realize his own mistakes. Irony did not become a goal for him, but appeared as a means of educating people in the spirit of moral values. After all, a critical attitude to one's behavior, showing it through irony, helps a person to give an account to himself on the basis of his daily life, experience and knowledge, to "measure" his morality on the basis of high moral standards, to turn a person's heart into a fortress of truth. The ironies of Socrates are characterized by the fact that that they served that purpose. Socratic satire became a means of changing objective reality, and Alloma gave impetus to the development of this tradition.

In general, from a communicative-pragmatic point of view, irony is a complex phenomenon, and it can be approached from different angles, assuming different goals and objectives. Therefore, it is sometimes artistic, sometimes linguistic, sometimes cultural, sometimes philosophical, sometimes cognitive, etc., to be considered as phenomena. No matter how it is viewed as a phenomenon, it is still impossible to explore and explore one side of this phenomenon, completely separated from the other. It is inconceivable that one side of irony could be presented without the other side, that it could be taken as a subject of research on the basis of the absolute negation of others. Therefore, it is advisable to approach irony based on the principle of dialectics "the variety of things." The original and true ontological essence of irony is restored on the basis of a generalization of conclusions about these aspects.

The cooperation of pragmatic factors with linguistic ones is of particular importance in characterizing the speech of an anthropocentric metaphor. They show their bright features in the relationship of harmony and adaptation.

Methodological features of literary texts, specific and genre features of the work are also external factors for the communicator. After all, when a writer is engaged in poetic creativity, he is obliged to follow the rules of the lyrical genre. Following these laws, requirements and principles of art does not depend on his will. This creates conditions for him to effectively use anthropocentric metaphors, depending on his speech intent. Conditions pragmatic factors: **The morning trembles in the arms of the late dawn, / The pink dawn extinguishes the stars. / My soul, my soul is in the knife of poetry... / The earth is my spell, the sky is my spell... Poetry is kindness!/ I suffered. On the wing of my mind** Raising the seas**I flew in search. / I saw many stars in my life / I saw stars in the sea. / I looked at the sky, my soul burned... / What mysteries are in the layers of clouds! / Sky, which kills me with amazement, / Mother Earth, fly away, let me go! / I said yor.. Lailimi or Shirinmi or! / Or some talent to be born? / Before my eyes appeared that "Here I am", / "Here I am", a single heart, nourished by poetry. / It will still be a world poem, Only knowing that it is useless, the arms of the world - / This world must be buried in secret, And the knife of poetry must be plunged into the heart !**So, we can say that in communication with "purely informational" content, metaphorical meanings are mainly of a linguistic nature, and in communication with the content "information + impact", occasional speech types are used..

The interaction of the pragmatic situation with linguistic factors in the speech implementation of anthropocentric metaphors plays an important role in the implementation of speech intent.

It is known that linguistic factors are of particular importance in the differentiation of the meanings of words according to the communicative plan. According to the linguist B. Mengliev, who conducted a special study on this subject, "when a lexeme is encountered in speech, generalization occurs on the basis of several intermediate "steps". Morphological and syntactic levels interact in the differentiation and implementation of these fragments, called intermediate lexical meanings, in which the ratio of their "contributions" is different. For example, a syntactic model introduces a lexeme into speech, a morphological tool forms it. However, sometimes syntax prevails, sometimes morphology in highlighting its intermediate lexical meanings. If syntax has the ability to introduce a lexeme into speech and highlight its intermediate lexical meanings, then morphology is limited to its formation. If the function of the syntactic model is limited to the introduction of a unit into speech, then the activity of morphology increases. Now he will be busy not only with the formation of a lexeme, but also with the differentiation of intermediate syllables.[107] Let's turn to examples. The generation that was born after the death of Raim the wrestler and grew up on rumors about him, which subsequently disappeared from their memory, began to build their houses from polished and baked bricks, and this house, which had once been the pride and beauty of tersota, suddenly became ugly, and now, like Momo Bayna, the house stands alone in front of the houses in the village, only the passing years, pressing each other, write sad inscriptions on the walls of the house, trying in vain to burn some distant memory in the restless heart of this generation, and this place, together with the mistress, has already lost its former power and dignity, forgotten and abandoned. wind"). Words separated in the text are used in a figurative sense, the word to beborn - "appear", the word to be "separate" - "separate", the word push means "with anxiety", the word "come" means "passing" , the word haste means "quickly". The main meaning of these words has an anthropocentric essence. The text expresses a metaphorical meaning based on the "man → existence" model.

---

[107] Mengliev B. Language as an integral system: Monograph. - Tashkent: Nihol, 2010. (-192 p.) - P.168.

These colloquial meanings of words are based on the general lexical meanings of the lexemes on which they are based, and the syntactic factor is leading in the differentiation and expression of certain meanings. That is, the words that are associated with them or associated with them help to read figurative meanings. At the same time, the nature of the text (that it is a literary text) also contributes to these linguistic factors. The meanings of these words in the text have a common aspect with an anthropocentric metaphorical meaning, and the unifying element is the tones of sadness and depression. This serves to bring out the mental state and mood of Bina Momo's character. Information about Baina Momo, who "spent in seclusion for almost fifty years, leaning on the pillars in this porch," also shows the figurative meaning of these words.

The communicative intention of the writer is to emphasize the transience of human life, the transience of life and the immortality of life, in which the human figure is a guest who comes and goes, thus he chooses effective means to warn the reader. He sets them an artistic and aesthetic task. To do this, Byna compares momo's house to herself, and momo to home. He builds "bridges" of similarities between completely dissimilar phenomena. He uses human qualities in the depiction of inanimate objects and inhuman qualities in the depiction of people. This prompted the reader, with the help of metaphorical models, to make a paradoxical philosophical conclusion that what has become of the house ends, even with a person as strong as metal, what is the life of a person, tender as a flower,

In the text, the intention of the writer-communicator, poetic skill, objective reality, the integrity of linguistic factors ensure the quality of communicative information and its effectiveness.

The pragmatic meaning can exaggerate certain aspects of a person without revealing his character, and in many cases can serve to express the feelings of the speaking communicator - to serve as an intention to influence. In this case, of course, it is necessary to have an appropriate pragmatic situation. Example:

- Baburzhon, why didn't you bring our bride? - he asked.

Botyr pretended not to hear. Norboy, walking behind, repeated his question.

- Baburzhon, why didn't you bring our bride?

And this time the hero pretended not to hear, and continued on his way.

We approached the car. Norboy, who was still following Beaubourjon like sticky glue, answered the question for the third time. After that, Momishuli stopped. He furrowed his brows, his mustache fanned out.

"Old pig, what are you going to do with your fiancee?" - said the hero, gritting his teeth.

Norboy trembled and turned pale.

"No... just... he was going to visit his relatives," the husband said with floating eyes.(Ch. Aitmatov, M. Shokhanov, "The hunter went to the top").

The inappropriate behavior of the listener-communicator prompted the speaker to use an anthropocentric metaphor to insult him.

old pig the entry of a complex compound into an imperative function, the use of the phrase "kelinni ki kelinni" in relation to the second person, shows that the word "kilinni" is used in the sentence, and the appeal to the expression old pig to man. But whether the expression corresponds to the designation is a subjective phenomenon. Because the auxiliary reasons for his speech realization were such factors as the verb and the mood of the speaking communicator. At the same time, the culture, level and nature of the listener's communication also played a special role in the emergence of metaphorical meaning as external factors. The metaphorical meaning is of a linguistic nature, and the word in this sense is applied to stupid people. As they say, the word comes from two hands, the speaking communicator could not translate this expression into the language, but keep it inside. But the listener given the personality of the speaker, this embarrassing situation could have been avoided even if he had observed the etiquette of private communication. The hearer's anticipation of the speaker's verb precludes any attempt to justify it.

In general, first of all, in this place, the factors of the listener and, moreover, the speaker are intensified, interacting with linguistic factors in harmony with the neutralized speech situation, helping the speaker to realize his intention to influence. At the same time, the author's speech, the author's communicative intention, although indirectly, does not leave its influence on the realization of the metaphorical meaning. True, when analyzing a text, when it comes to communicants entering into a dialogue, in certain cases it is necessary to artificially ignore the author of the text. But even in this case, the author's aesthetic ideal and worldview leave traces in the communicative situation of the text. Therefore, it is necessary to rely on the author's component, without giving it priority in the analysis.

As mentioned above, in the speech implementation of a metaphorical meaning, internal and external factors are somehow combined with linguistic factors. The internal (personal) factor refers to the communicators and their characteristics, which are the driving force behind the communication process.

The personal factor is characterized by extreme complexity. It is determined both by the complexity of the personality and by many aspects of the personality. Also, since the organizer of the dialogue is a person, he differs primarily in his activity in comparison with other factors. Below we will consider the place and role of important aspects of the personality factor in the realization of metaphorical meaning in the section of other factors.

Intention Factor. Communication is a diverse phenomenon characterized by the relativity of its constituent types of sentences (declarative sentences, interrogative sentences, imperative sentences). Its relativity can be substantiated as follows. First, sentences have no purpose, but the speaker's purpose is revealed through words. Secondly, it is not recommended to force all operators into these three types. Since an indicative sentence can have the form or content of a question or command, an interrogative sentence can be the content of an indicative or imperative sentence, and an imperative sentence can be the form or content of an indicative or interrogative sentence. This is one side of the matter. In addition, the range of interests and interests of a person is very wide, and they can manifest themselves in different forms. For example:

They say that every time has its own scale,

Oh, how true is this great truth. (A. Oripov)

These sentences are similar in form to traditional sentences. But the purpose of providing information about the unknown is not felt in it. It seems that the content of the message is rather unclear. This ambiguity arises on the basis of a different intention of the speaker. The speaker expresses his mood and excitement on the basis of reemphasizing an existing and known fact. A demonstration is a pragmatic situation mixed with artistic intent. The goal to express excitement, to share feelings prompted these lines to be put on paper.

Of course, it is necessary to rank goals. The proposal itself contains a set of goals, one of which requires the other, and the other requires the third. "O.G. Pocheptsov notes that the action of the initial goal corresponds mainly to the structural and semantic features of the sentence. Therefore, "How to get to the station?" The initial intentional act of the speech structure is a request, and the structure "Today there was a meeting at the university" is an indication, if it consists in saying: "Give me back my book!" In the structure, the initial intention is unconditional, an order, a requirement. But the emerging target actions, firstly, are numerous, and secondly, the structural and semantic structure of the sentence does not matter to them. The formation of the resulting intention is associated not only with the semantic features of sentences, but also with the environment of their activation, with the speech context. In other words, an action followed by a goal,[108]In fact, the words "I have come" are clearly figurative. This is also indicated by its grammatical form. At the same time, the speaker asked: "What is your mission for me?" asks a question. "Information sharing activities are not limited to a simple message or request. The performance of these actions is aimed at meeting the demand and interest of the addressee and the addressee. This is a pragmatic task. So, in the evening communication, pragmatic tasks are realized within the framework of the communicative goal. Therefore, the perlocutionary effect resulting from a speech act is better included in the framework of

---

[108]Safarov Sh. Recommended works. - B. 74-75.

pragmalinguistic analysis.[109] In this case, linguistic expressions are only in the status of clothes, and the pragmatic situation can show the purpose of the sentence, the intention of the speaker. "Under the intention of speech is understood the establishment of transmission over a channel of a certain connection, established in a physical speech signal by means of linguistic signs."[110]

Representation of anthropomorphic metaphors in literary texts. The "dance of metaphors" occurs in speech when the speaker's intention is not to inform, but to influence. In particular, anthropocentric metaphors perform the intentional task of increasing impressionability, exaggerating reality, and increasing expressiveness. In particular, some examples of anthropomorphic metaphors can be found in the following verse:

Oh, you mountains, how beautiful! /
The sun will give you the first light.

Feather clouds, pearly snows/
    Head on high. /
    ShohShola Tashar shouted, /*
    Give beauty to your breasts./
    Hitting his head on the rocks, /
    A flood overflowing with water./

The text uses five anthropomorphic metaphors. Adib did not set himself the goal of providing information about the features of nature. Perhaps in an effort to show the artistic intent of creating an impressive poetic image. When you read a poem, it is as if nature has been given a soul, and everything in it has a human quality in its

---

[109]Safarov Sh. Recommended works. -B. 85-86.
[110]Susov I.P. Introduction to the study of languages: a textbook for students of linguo-philological specialties /I.P. Thirst. - M.: AST: East-West, 2007. - 379 p. - S. 79.

behavior. When we approach a text from a general point of view, the emotional intention is higher than the communicative intention. Because getting new information directly from the text is much weaker than getting artistic pleasure. The reason we use the word "weak" instead of "no new information" is that it is still possible to look for communicative information and, if necessary, find it. For example, it is impossible to refute the information that that the blows of water against rocks are analogous to the blows of a man's head. In addition, giving the quality of "magnificent" to the waterfall is an artistic principle, means to note the similarity in notation. It seems that all comparisons used in poetic texts are intended to convey the wisdom of harmony between the phenomena of being. In ordinary conversation, for example, it is not customary to make such comparisons. This shows that the literary text is a pragmatic factor.

Thoughts about the embodiment of wisdom, beauty and kindness in any high-level literary text allow us to understand a new qualitative view of communicative information and the intention in them.

Worldview factor. In the application of anthropocentric metaphorical expressions, in other words, the level of communicators plays an important role in their implementation. The speaker's worldview is manifested in his use of metaphorical models. For example, there is no connection between maple and the Silk Road. But the conflicts in his mood are transferred to his language. In it we see the combined state of the poles of burning and laughter. The writer expresses this with the help of contrasting metaphors:

The soul of the Batyr sect is bitter. Batyr burned the body of the sect. The soul of the batyr sect... rejoiced.

"Comrade Rashidov..." he breathed. - Sharof Rashidovich, the maples we planted... It has become the Great Silk Road, the Great Silk Road!

Inside the batyr sect was on fire. The inner part of the hero laughed...

– Comrade Rashidov... the gardens we created... have become the Great Silk Road, the Great Silk Road!

There was sadness in the eyes of the Hero Sect. It was a holiday in the eyes of the batyr faction...

- Comrade Rashidov... we will now walk along the Great Silk Road. The Great Silk Road leads us to the world. Istanbul, Paris, London...

Adib Batyr wants to give away the sarcasm stuck in his throat: "The path to the future is closed for us," when he says that we will go along the Great Silk Road through gardens and maples. It seems to you that the worldview of a person from an ordinary background can give such uninteresting metaphors. But he, perhaps without knowing it himself, said something and revealed his artistic intention. So, the worldview of batyr Koshchi served as a tool for the artistic embodiment of the writer's communicative intention.

mood factor. Good/unpleasant mood is realized by the personal factor. When a person is in high spirits, they use more metaphorical expressions with a positive meaning, while a depressed mood leads to the manifestation of metaphors with a negative connotation mixed with sad tones: "Like an orphaned bush on the road of a great caravan / Tears in the eyes of anticipation ..." / My lord, man, is it really not in your hands, / My lord, why don't you raise your head. / Blind, evil death, a thousand dods from your hand, / Have you entered the field of poetry, like darkness. / Death. , did you really pierce with a spear / The warrior of Uzbek poetry. / She went to distant lands and returned, Even the setting sun could not rise.

The words "head" and "liver" used in the text of the poem, of course, are not used in their meaning. Or the fact that the sun will rise, not knowing its fate, is peculiar only to people. The author's appeal to music is much higher and more impressive than the dictionary meaning of the word "play": "Why, my homeland will be forgiven / Today Gafur Gulyam is forever at the beginning? / For the first time, maybe my liver fluttered, / Lol, the words did not come from my stiff language. / Cry, my mother, my homeland, / You don't have a child today, / Sick music, your moans one after another, / Cry yourself, oh, sadness in your heart The world is crying hard, and the world is crying without finding a solution. (Abdulla Oripov)

On the contrary, in texts written in high spirits, we find metaphorical expressions in high flight:At the very foot of the Hissar Mountains/ There is a place of good air, calm, high./ This is a strange sky, under the sky./ The stars seem like this, if you stretch out your hand./ This place is a beautiful art of mother nature, This is the realm of man and stars./ Here passes belt of the earth, / Begasamton means that it is a colorful earth. / When the stars shine in the sky / The image of a sharp Uzbek is ready. / This is a beautiful place named after Ulugbek, / This is one fifth of the observatory in the world. (Abdulla Oripov)

Ethical factor. A person's behavior is also reflected in his speech. You can evaluate the inner world of a person and moral qualities by his speech. Moral qualities are important when using anthropocentric metaphors within the personal factor. There are no deviations from the norms of morality in the speech of people with positive behavior. They retain their individuality even in difficult situations:

Hadji came to Kumush's head and killed him. Otabek and his mother got to their feet, Kumush's eyes were closed, his hair was tousled over his face. Hadji straightened his hair with his own hands, saw Kumush's pale face and clenched his fist...

- Mother ... Mother! .. - said the pilgrim. Opening her silver eyes, Grandma looked at her and recognized... she wanted to move.

- Don't move, mom... don't move!

Kumush's tears flowed from his temple... Hadji could not resist, wiped Kumush's tears and stroked his head:

- God heals, my child!

Kumush went up to the silver bowl, Otabek came up and hugged him, the pilgrim also grabbed his head...

Sociolinguistic possibilities of anthropomorphic metaphors should be studied not only in artistic, but also in scientific, official, journalistic discourses. The formation of metaphors is influenced by various factors.

In particular, the poetic metaphor of Sh. Rahman has not yet been fully reflected in linguistic works. Many researchers of Sh. Rahman's poetry (linguists and literary critics) pay attention to the abundance of other linguistic means in the creative heritage of the poet: nature - man, night - day, speech - silence, etc. Is there a genesis of these conflicts, or are there no clear boundaries mutual negation in the world of Sh. Rahman's poetry? The answer to this question is directly related to the study of metaphor, since it has the ability to harmonize, find similarities and unite things belonging to different taxonomic classes. N. D. Arutyunova is also a "classical metaphor" - a synthesis term in the field of analysis, representation (image) of a common "country", "class" in relation to the zone of imagination in the field of a separate mind in the world.[111]said.

The world in which metaphor plays an important role is determined by modern trends in linguistic studies of the landscape of the Uzbek language. For example, in Russian linguistics, the originality of Tyutchev's poetry as a product of mental activity is most clearly manifested as a result of the identification and comprehensive analysis of the main conceptual metaphors in his poetic language. Such an analysis allows us to determine the level of knowledge of the structure of the poetic linguistic personality of F. I. Tyutchev, which plays an important role in describing the poet's idiostyle. F. Ya. The depth of the metaphorical image in Tyutchev's poetry is a feature. Tyutchev, first of all, determines the implementation of his philosophical and mythopoetic views on the relationship between nature and man. The development of generative semantics in the 60s of the 20th century was based on the cognitive function of metaphor, communicative, emotional,[112]). Firstly, to analyze the various definitions of metaphor, and secondly, to outline the history of the study of metaphor, starting from the works of ancient philosophers and ending with modern linguistic dictionaries.

Already in ancient Greek rhetoric, it was argued that metaphor is an objective sign of language and speech, and the very phenomenon of metaphor is a product of empirical understanding of the world by a person. Metaphor is the use of a word or phrase in a language to refer to an object, understood as conveying a portion of a previous meaning.

Russian science of the 18th century gives the traditional definition of metaphor (the transfer of meaning by analogy). M. V.

---

[111] N. D. Arutyunova. Metaphor and discourse. The theory is metaphorical. - M., 1990. - p. 5-32.
[112] Lakoff D., Johnson M. The metaphor I live by. In: Language and modeling of social interaction. - M.: Progress, 1987.

Lomonosov developed not only the classification of metaphors, but also the rules for using this trope in speech. Metaphor in Russian linguistics began to be systematically studied only in the 20th century. A. A. Potebney deepened the theory of metaphor: he developed the mechanisms of formation and action of metaphor, syntactic and semantic classification. At the end of the 19th century, N. M. Krushevsky wrote about the associative nature of metaphor and focused it on psychological phenomena.

The twentieth century was a period of development of the doctrine of metaphor. The views of scientists are moving from studying the aesthetic potential of this linguistic phenomenon to its cognitive and pragmatic functions. A. Richare, M. Black, S. Pepper and E. Researchers such as Cormack describe the mechanism of metaphor formation from the standpoint of psycholinguistics and highlight the main metaphors.

The study of metaphor in Russian linguistics of the twentieth century is aimed at studying its semantic potential in the artistic language. V. V. In the works of Vinogradov, G. O. Vinokur, there is an opinion that there is no such linguistic phenomenon that would not function in poetic speech. Scientists conclude that metaphorization is a process of semantic transformations based on the intersection of different semantic fields.

The second half of the 20th century - the beginning of the 21st century is a period of active formation of cognitive and conceptual hypotheses about the mechanisms of metaphorization. The central works of this period in world linguistics are J. R. Tolkien's Studies. Lakoff and M. Johnson, J. Fauconnier and M. Linguists such as Turner consider metaphor as a mental rather than a purely linguistic category. So, the theory of conceptual integration is an improved conceptual theory of J. R. Tolkien, the essence of which is metaphorization - the construction of one semantic space into another on the basis of "terms". What is new is that a person, as a linguistic person, does not just control the metaphor, but the metaphor, which is a logical and psychological category, makes him look at the world in a certain way.

In the internal metaphorology of this period, N.D. Arutyunova. in his opinion, language is anthropocentric, and therefore a person becomes the starting point in the analysis of linguistic phenomena. N. D. Arutyunova gives a detailed functional classification of metaphors, paying attention to the level of "solidity" of such language units. G.N. Sklyarevskaya mainly identifies a number of semantic fields involved in the process of metaphorization, three of which are associated with a person.

Thus, at the present stage of the development of metaphorology, we see that a person, his language, mentality and psychology are at the center of linguistic research.

One of the most interesting contexts in which metaphors function is poetry. The peculiarity of the poetic language is that it most clearly reveals the semantic potential of language units, therefore the poetic landscapes of the world are logically different from each other. Here the metaphor serves as a tool for understanding and reconstructing the world.

From this point of view, the research interest is not the metaphorization of the author, but the specific representation of metaphorical models in the common language in the artistic heritage of the author.

Metaphor is a means of understanding new conceptual areas in areas closer to direct physical experience. The aim of anthropocentric research is the study of man in language and man in language.

The poetry of Shavkat Rahman as a research material on Uzbek linguistics can be used as a reflection of his metaphorical thinking, directly in the implementation of the concept of metaphor anthropomorphism in poetic speech. Taking into account the structural-semantic classification of metaphors presented here, in which heterotopic problems are developed in the poetry of Shavkat Rahman, the language highlighted in the general patterns of his phraseology are the works of Shavkat Rahman can be set as a relation.

The lexeme usually, that is, out of context, has two meanings: firstly, displeasure, displeasure, softly, but very openly expressed; secondly, dull, vaguely noisy. In the context we are considering, the meaning of the connection is close to the first. If we look at the whole context of Shaukat Rahman (the metaphor is repeated), we will catch some meanings. The expansion of the context introduces additional semantic shades. The author describes the sound content of the noise: sometimes it sounds wonderful, then it fades again. So, according to the observations of many researchers, the indicator of uncertainty (lexical combination) in Shaukat Rahman: wonderful sounds are sounds that can flood or shake the soul. Let us turn once again to the issue of semantics: this means both the loudness of the sound and the degree of its impact on the soul of the poet.

The metaphor in formation is primarily based on the intersection of associative lines, which we can observe in the example. The semantics are very specific and ambiguous, which allows for interpretation.

Two-dimensionality is, on the one hand, a metaphor, on the other, a feature that combines figurativeness and associativity. In metaphor, two qualitative systems interact, and the image is also created by the poet. When two events are compared, and finally, associations link ideas about two realities.

The expressiveness of such metaphors is due, first of all, to the fact that the image creates two series of associations associated simultaneously with direct and figurative meaning, for example: *There are no sparks in the sky,// The mountains gave a clear belly, the green valley - with bright colors, I burned the bosom of the nights, mocked at the fetid lakes.//*(Eternal, 188). Here the metaphor is used to describe two realities at the same time:*pure snow*And*green valley - bright flowers*. The quality of clear is used in the literal sense: white, pure. The metaphor describing the vague, scattered light of the moon, the play of the colors of the night sky, simultaneously represents the fading waters of the river and the view of the general space surrounding the lyrical hero. The charm of a lexeme, which is interpreted as an attractive force emanating from someone or something, characterizes the author's reaction to what is happening, his impression.

Therefore, from this point of view, there is a confusion of associations associated with the literal meaning of the word pallor and the figurative word charm.

If the same metaphor is used to describe the same objects in different contexts, this becomes a semantic contrast. In this case, of course, speech attracts the attention of the addressee, delays it, activates the memory and imagination of the reader. So, in the poetic works of Sh. Rahman, one can find the following examples of such metaphors that create an idea of quiet, obscure sounds that createimage of spring: Now the saffron nights are white / glorious holding torches / walking through the beautiful expanses / looking for spring days. / (Sh. Rahman.32).

In these contexts, the spring element has speech incomprehensible to man, but understandable to the world. The constant appeal of the poet to the image shows that there is something important in it for its creator. Through the poetry of Sh. Rahman, we can confirm this: A dream floats in the mountains... / Cancer will leave the Aloy mountains, / The cold winds have awakened. in the stream, we'll take a bath. / We sleep until midnight, / We count the mysterious stars. Analyzing the poet's verses, it becomes clear that he refers to the image of the mountain many times. In fact, his poems have a metaphorical meaning, that is, they express figurative meanings.

The mountain in the poetry of the poet is the sublime spirit of the poet, the joy of suffering. This is probably why the mountains live with him from the first poems of the poet to the last: The mountain sighed heavily - / The wind rushed into the valleys, / The crescent moon hid its faces. / The mountain sighed heavily, the heart woke up from a deep sleep, / It is necessary to sigh like the mountains.

The theme of the mountain is also present in his last poems: Nadirajan, Shoirajan, / My body does not move, / Call my mountains from distant oases / The sky is full of air / One is not enough for me ... / Nadirajan, Shoirajan / My body does not move, / It snows . To the mountains: / they say the poet lies, / In God's yard ... / The sky is full of air / It's not enough for me ... /

All this was attachment to the motherland, the motherland, love inseparable from it. The poet skillfully expressed his feelings using metaphors. "Call my mountains from distant oases" definitely applies to people.

Mountains Shavkat occupies an important place in the poetry of Rahman. Moreover, the Aloy ranges are not at all like other mountains. Reminds me of giant snowdrops. We seem to be surprised at the power of nature when we see stones cut into layers with sharp knives. The names are also surprising: Ketmontog, Kettantog, Ettantog, Eshiktosh, Beshiktosh. Since his childhood was spent mainly in the mountains, Shavkat Rahman often refers to the mountains: The mountains - the Northui are gone forever, / Chewing and chewing dry years. / Where are the hooves, hooves, where are the chests with gold and jewelry? / A robbed old man who hid the traces of robbers / ./ paws of hidden years/ the voice of the murderer who killed the sarban./ the place of metaphor in the poet's poetry can be clearly understood from the text of this poem.

"The opposite way of introducing metaphor into a text is that different metaphors express the same subject in different contexts and create a polyphony of meanings. - in addition, it carries a significant expressive charge, determines the reader's deep experience of this image. For example, in many poems by Sh. Rahman there is an image of the speech of the night world, incomprehensible to a person, when the whole space is filled with vague sounds that can only be felt in a dream. There is no clear definition of this phenomenon anywhere. We can extract some of its properties only by summing the values of different containers. It depends on the ability of a metaphor to construct new concepts based on existing ones by crossing, overlaying, gluing associative lines, to synthesize new things that do not yet exist in the real world. Are the flowers stones when thousands of caltabins / walk around and fall, / I said with a brave smile, you'll see, / someday this stone, of course, will bloom. , even the keen eyes of the poet do not see these flowers... / - the chosen metaphors are caused by the interaction of the same concepts: a sharp eye, a flowering stone. On the basis of the associative series formed from these dominants, a system for describing non-existent poetic reality is built. flowering stone. On the basis of the associative series formed from these dominants, a system for describing non-existent poetic reality is built. flowering stone. On the basis of the associative series formed from these dominants, a system for describing non-existent poetic reality is built.

Thus, Sh. Rahman's poetic metaphor is mainly based on various associations - emotional and abstract, intellectual and emotional. They connect the empirical and life experience of the student, activate his imagination, make the image bright, visible and therefore expressive.

The expressiveness of such metaphors is connected, first of all, with the fact that the image creates two series of associations associated with direct and figurative meaning at the same time, for example: there are sharp words left, / If there are no sharp words left.. Nothing will remain (Sh. Rahman 188). Here the metaphor is used to describe two realities at the same time: sharp words and sharp words. The lexeme charm, interpreted as an attractive force emanating from someone or something, sufficiently characterizes the author's reaction to what is happening, his impression.

Therefore, from this point of view, there is a confusion of associations associated with the literal meaning of the word sharp and the figurative word charm.

If the same metaphor is used to describe the same objects in different contexts, this becomes a semantic contrast. In this case, of course, speech attracts the attention of the addressee, delays it, activates the memory and imagination of the reader. So, in the poetic works of Sh. Rahman, one can find the following examples of such metaphors that create an idea of the quiet, obscure sounds created by spring landscapes:*Spring believes in you, look, / his heart swam into his eyes, - /looking for you waiting, / you must love spring. / Look at him, do not drive him away - / do not make the thousandth mistake. /***Won't leave your doorstep*** *in the spring, / until you return to your source. / East **Asov months**, / Colors waft from his breath, / He plays **green birds** burning flowers...*

"The opposite way of introducing metaphor into a text is that different metaphors express the same subject in different contexts and create a polyphony of meanings. In addition, it carries a significant expressive charge, determines the reader's deep experience of this image.

Thus, Sh. Rahman's poetic metaphor is mainly based on various associations - emotional and abstract, intellectual and emotional. They connect the empirical and life experience of the student, activate his imagination, make the image bright, visible and therefore expressive.

Metaphorical knowledge can go in two directions: general language and "lyrical" (that is, the use of metaphor in poetic texts in a cognitive function). The path of vernacular includes understanding the world on the basis of empirically acquired knowledge by a person of an objective nature. In this case, the metaphor serves as a conductor from one segment of experience to another; it is not a direct means of cognition, but connects all available information. As a result of such thinking, a person understands the real world. At the heart of the "lyrical" direction is the knowledge not of reality, but of the unique world created by the poet himself. Here the metaphor most fully fulfills the function of cognition, since it is a means of creating objects of poetic reality. This is a wide path, because the poet does not collect the qualities of one object, but creates new ones.

The peculiarity of Sh. Rahman's metaphorization lies in the fact that he uses the method of intensive cognition "common language" in the lyrical text. A narrow circle of topics is focused on the main binary categories, distinguished by their belonging to two worlds: earthly and heavenly. The metaphor in this case is linear. A random image begins to develop with features borrowed from other metaphors. This feature can be illustrated by analyzing the evolution of one metaphor. It is known that *Floats and shines / Shards of the moon in the blue waters. / An icy wind arrives - /old mountain **sighs**i./ Blows in the neck of mint / lush valleys run into the valley./ The ponds are covered/ the toads cover the silence./ The veins of the earth heat up.../ Warm heights spread out into the night./ Suddenly Hot Summer flows through the silent gardens./*in his poem*in a particular case (old mountain **sighs** And **fragments of the moon**, lush valleys, Hot Summe* retc.) are vivid examples of metaphor, in particular, anthropomorphic metaphor.

The following metaphor also reflects the poet's impressions of spring:*Green tree in the morning / my window pressed his face on the surface of the glass, as on glass - / he gently wrote his flowers. / A rustling breeze flew in, / Striving for, rejoicing, /Spring, the body opens and shines, / A fog of spirits envelops it. / As if the sun has split ... / The world drowns with joy. / Not every spring it melts in me /tree that teaches to live./ (Sh. Rahman, 89.)*

Anthropomorphic metaphor also played an important role in creating a special language of Sh. Rahman's poetry.

The connotative meaning is more clearly reflected when conveying meaning through metaphor. For example, there are lexemes with the names of animals and birds, such as horse, donkey, sheep, dog, wolf, fox, tiger, owl, owl, eagle, falcon, swallow, nightingale. These words are very widely used in a figurative sense. apart from their meaning. Typical characteristics such as the strength of a horse, the stupidity of a donkey, the meekness of a sheep, the loyalty of a dog, the dexterity of a cat, the cunning of a fox, the strength of an eagle's grip, the sharpness of the mind. hawk's eye are metaphorically transferred to other objects, resulting in a connotative meaning, and the effectiveness of the text increases.

Our linguists have expressed their opinion on the difference between a metaphor and a construction of comparison. They mainly list the following differences:

1. In comparison, words take part in their meaning. 2. In comparison, two components are compared - the object of comparison and the image of comparison. The metaphor is one-component. 3. Comparisons have a lot of scope for expansion, a sentence can expand even at the paragraph level. Metaphors are made up of words or phrases. 4. There are special indicators in comparisons: -dec, -day, -simon, -larcha, kabi, like. This can be seen from the following example: Karim is a cunning fox. Comparison is a construction in which Karim is the subject of comparison, the fox is the standard of comparison, the trickster is the basis of comparison, and the day is a formal indicator of comparison. This is the perfect analogy. Karim is a fox. This is an abbreviated comparison because the sentence does not specify the basis of comparison (which feature is similar) and the indicator. Oh, the fox... (Used in relation to Karim). This is a metaphor. Because Karim's cunning is figuratively expressed,

completely renamed. Examples of metaphors: 1. Donkey, what have you done? 2. The "telegraph" of prisons (talker, spy) works very well. 3. "He was stabbed in the chest," said the barracks officer. - Make it worse! Death of a dog to a dog. The prisoners won't let him live anyway. 4. - A fly got into the soup, brother! - he said timidly... Dvorovaya Gazeta has arrived. 5. Crows left over from the winter. 6. Meeting with a buffalo. (S. Ahmad). 7. Otabek recognized this meadow janitor and noticed his sarcasm. (A. Kadiri). Because Karim's cunning is figuratively expressed, completely renamed. Examples of metaphors: 1. Donkey, what have you done? 2. The "telegraph" of prisons (talker, spy) works very well. 3. "He was stabbed in the chest," said the barracks officer. - Make it worse! Death of a dog to a dog. The prisoners won't let him live anyway. 4. - A fly got into the soup, brother! - he said timidly... Dvorovaya Gazeta has arrived. 5. Crows left over from the winter. 6. Meeting with a buffalo. (S. Ahmad). 7. Otabek recognized this meadow janitor and noticed his sarcasm. (A. Kadiri). Because Karim's cunning is figuratively expressed, completely renamed. Examples of metaphors: 1. Donkey, what have you done? 2. The "telegraph" of prisons (talker, spy) works very well. 3. "He was stabbed in the chest," said the barracks officer. - Make it worse! Death of a dog to a dog. The prisoners won't let him live anyway. 4. - A fly got into the soup, brother! - he said timidly... Dvorovaya Gazeta has arrived. 5. Crows left over from the winter. 6. Meeting with a buffalo. (S. Ahmad). 7. Otabek recognized this meadow janitor and noticed his sarcasm. (A. Kadiri). The prisoners won't let him live anyway. 4. - A fly got into the soup, brother! - he said timidly... Dvorovaya Gazeta has arrived. 5. Crows left over from the winter. 6. Meeting with a buffalo. (S. Ahmad). 7. Otabek recognized this meadow janitor and noticed his sarcasm. (A. Kadiri). The prisoners won't let him live anyway. 4. - A fly got into the soup, brother! - he said timidly... Dvorovaya Gazeta has arrived. 5. Crows left over from the winter. 6. Meeting with a buffalo. (S. Ahmad). 7. Otabek recognized this meadow janitor and noticed his sarcasm. (A. Kadiri).

Some sources speak of three types of metaphors by content: conventional, animating and synesthetic metaphors. All the metaphors discussed above are basically conditional metaphors. Animation is one of the important means of giving figurativeness to artistic speech. The authors of the book Visual Arts put it this way: "Animation is a form of metaphor. Animation is a method of depiction that arises by transferring the characteristics of people to inanimate objects, natural phenomena, animals, poultry, birds. In the "stylistics of the Uzbek language" this means "the transfer of actions, feelings, speech and thoughts of a person to inanimate objects." it is emphasized that this is called revitalization. In our classical literature, two types of revitalization are distinguished:

1. Diagnostics- a personification depicting inanimate objects in the form of people. In poetry, animation is used to describe reality figuratively. This technique is used to bring the reader closer to the object of the image, to facilitate understanding of reality, to avoid a dry and colorless expression.

In the following poetic passage, the author activates the reader's reaction to the depicted reality, enlivening "autumn":

What do I want? What do I want?
I listen to the noise of the meadow.
Quietly wandering in the strip of leaves
I see a gloomy and restless autumn.
In his song, in his mind
Sometimes I feel the human heart.(A. Oripov).

Or treating an inanimate object as if it were addressing a person is also a form of animation. In the literature, this phenomenon is called an apostrophe. In this case, things do not come to life, but only appear alive. This method is used to reveal the inner pains and secrets of the hero, which he could not tell anyone about. For example: Trees reaching for the sky, knowing that your roots are in the earth, do you desire the blue breast that came and hugged you? Don't you feel that every spring the greenery deceives you, or do you obey the wind and rustle, knowing everything and feeling everything. I whisper too... The dew falling on you is my tear... I know that even if I cannot pour out all my pain, it is because of my helpless state. After all, you are a living memory. The whisper of your lonely leaves, the song of the mournful rain, the bending grasses, the capricious wind, the sighs of plague, the indefatigable farmer of my heart, you, my simple trees, and the chaos of the sky, which I did not know how to bend - we are all bound by lonely longing. (Yu. Akram).

2. Wait- it means to characterize as a speaker, to speak like people. Intok is often used in nursery rhymes and stories, fairy tales and parables. The art of speech is used in parables for a specific purpose. Some human defects are figuratively shown as examples of defects.

In European literary criticism, the so-called allegory is also based on the method of "speaking". In the animation of things and objects, animals talk like people. In allegorical animation, animals and creatures act like people, speak like them. The reader focuses on the image of a person depicted through these animals. So, in an allegory, the system of images is two lines, that is, a line of images of animals depicted in a work, and through them a line of people of a given character. In the fable of Mukhtar Khudoykulov called "Fly with the Lion", the pride characteristic of some people, the vice of striving to gain authority, even if it is a lie, is figuratively expressed: the fly sat down on the Lion's ear for a moment and flew away. . Then he boasted of what appeared: - We are very close with Cher,

In synesthetic metaphors, a concept perceived by one sense organ is compared with a concept-thing perceived by another sense organ, and on this basis a figurative meaning is created. For example: Sweet smile, sweet speech, sweet thought; such as a light smile, a light look, a light step, a heavy dream, a heavy word, a heavy deed. The synesthetic metaphor occurs in the adjectives "sweet", "light", and "heavy" in these examples. The words "sweet", meaning taste, and "light", meaning measure, came in the meaning of "pleasant", and the word "heavy" in the meaning of "unpleasant".

Metonymy It is said that meaning is conveyed on the basis of mutual proximity and connection between events and things. Metonymy is also based on comparison. Only in metaphor, when the signs of similar objects are compared, in metonymy, although these two objects have some connection with each other in their appearance or internal characteristics, they are completely different from each other (not similar to each other). object symbols are mixed. For example: ... with an unpleasant speech, good or bad, it is better to wait a little ... Fuzuli must be read carefully. (A. Kadiri). In this sentence, based on the relationship between the author and his works, "work" is renamed by the author's name. Or; The palace sleeps peacefully, midnight (A. Kadiri). In this example, the word "palace" also means "people in the palace". There are various forms of metonymy, and detailed information can be found in the literature on linguistics. We would like to recommend Mansoura to you. In it you will see the author's skillful use of metonymic renamings: "Reading

Hemingway - Brother Hemingway also struck me," said the poet from Bukhara. - Now I read Jabron Khali, Faulkner, Frisch. I came home that day. I again visited the worlds of Ernst, which I liked very much. It's right. Even Hemingway can beat Bad. It's too far if you see your free will. If your trust is broken Reading Hemingway - Brother Hemingway also struck me, - said the poet from Bukhara. - Now I read Jabron Khali, Faulkner, Frisch. I came home that day. I again visited the worlds of Ernst, which I liked very much. It's right. Even Hemingway can beat Bad. It's too far if you see your free will. If your trust is broken Reading Hemingway - Brother Hemingway also struck me, - said the poet from Bukhara. - Now I read Jabron Khali, Faulkner, Frisch. I came home that day. I again visited the worlds of Ernst, which I liked very much. It's right. Even Hemingway can beat Bad. It's too far if you see your free will. If your trust is broken

If it's like a deposit, it's worth it. Hemingway, teacher of manners. To noble treatment. And we are moving further and further away from such treatment.(I.G. Afurov).

Synecdoche it is considered to convey a value based on a whole-part relationship. It is possible to create synecdoches using the singular instead of the plural, or the plural instead of the singular in literature. said. The trees turned yellow, the apple tree blossomed, I cut off my hand, a piece with the name of the whole; The whole is expressed by the name of the part in such combinations as "poking your nose into every business", "hard to the marrow of the bones", "the hand of the collective is high". In artistic speech, synecdoche is used to ensure conciseness and expressiveness.

Irony to my translation, which consists in using a language unit in a sense opposite to its true meaning, with kesatik, kochirim, piching They say. Irony has long been used in our literature to create spectacular expressions.

In European literary criticism, this phenomenon is summarized by the term "irony". Its manifestations are called antiphrase (mockery, denial of one or another positive feature through laughter, sarcasm) and sarcasm (poisonous reproach, sarcastic insult, hint). Rare examples of irony can be found in the works of Abdullah Kahkhor, a master of words, an honored writer of our people. He created unique images using various forms of irony in comic stories and feuilletons, such as "The Woman Who Didn't Eat Raisins", "The Literature Teacher", "Speech". For example, Mulla Norkozi, depicted in ironic colors in the writer's story "The Woman Who Didn't Eat Raisins," is one of these characters: "Ayo; If a man shakes a man's hand and asks, that's it! his fast is broken - he can enjoy this mouthwash! I saw with my own eyes how the son of the master Mavlon gave a handful of raisins to the daughter of Abdulhakim. Do they have life? The Sharia way is the right way. At the age of eleven, wash the hands of a girl who did not cover her veil and hit her armpit. A veil is a veil of modesty!"

Paraphrase so-called pictorial expressions are considered as methodological means that ensure the emotional and expressiveness of artistic speech. Paraphrase is defined as "the expression of a thing, an event, not by its name, but in a descriptive way based on its characteristic features." It should not be forgotten that the name of an event-thing with a different phrase does not give the expected effect. There must be a meaningful proximity between the named event and the new name-phrase. For example, pilots are celestial falcons, a shark is an underwater ruler, a lion is a sultan of animals,

Samarkand is a gate of the East, a theater is a center of spirituality, youth is a time of love.

Exaggeration, grotesque and understatement. Exaggeration (or hyperbole) is an exaggerated description of things, events, feelings and characteristics. Exaggeration also serves to make the image impressive and expressive. Although the fact that the exaggeration is based on a shift in the meaning of the word indicates that it belongs to the group of tropes, it differs from other manifestations of the trope. Because in other forms of the trope, the figurative meaning is based on a known sign, comparison, comparison, event, or connection between objects, and exaggeration correctly requires not understanding in the sense of ri. Movement based on exaggeration is introduced into a literary text in order to draw the attention of the listener or reader to the subject of speech and provide emotional expressiveness of speech. Information expressed with exaggeration naturally does not correspond to the reality of life. But if the norm is violated, the expected effect may not be achieved. In fact, the main purpose of exaggerated speech is not to inform, but to influence the listener or reader. For example, in the following passage, the writer managed to create a comic effect by exaggerating the portrait of the hero: "In our area there lived a giant named Mamajon Lomboz. He was not very tall, but if he was a quarter of an inch wide, he was over two feet. When he sat down, his buttocks swelled like a cake and formed a three-gas circle. His stomach was so sagging that when he sat down on the ground, he went to the place of the blanket. When his navel itched, he could not reach it, so he scratched it with a fire shovel. (S. Ahmad). the main purpose of exaggerated speech is not to inform, but to influence the listener or reader. For example, in the next passage, the writer managed to create a comic effect by exaggerating the portrait of the hero: "In our area there lived a giant named Mamajon Lomboz. He was not very tall, but if he was a quarter of an inch wide, he was over two feet. When he sat down, his buttocks swelled like a cake and formed a three-gas circle. His stomach was so sagging that when he sat down on the ground, he went to the place of the blanket. When his navel itched, he could not reach it, so he scratched it with a fire shovel. (S. Ahmad). the main purpose of exaggerated speech is not to inform, but to influence the listener or reader. For example, in the following passage, the writer managed to create a comic effect by exaggerating the portrait of the hero: "In our area there lived a giant named Mamajon Lomboz. He was not very tall, but if he was a quarter of an inch wide, he was over two feet. When he sat down, his buttocks swelled like a cake and formed a three-gas circle. His stomach was so sagging that when he sat down on the ground, he went to the place of the blanket. When his navel itched, he could not reach it, so he scratched it with a fire shovel. (S. Ahmad). in the next passage, the writer managed to create a comic effect by exaggerating the portrait of the hero: "In our area there lived a giant named Mamajon Lomboz. He was not very tall, but if he was a quarter of an inch wide, he was over two feet. When he sat down, his buttocks swelled like a cake and formed a three-gas circle. His stomach was so sagging that when he sat down on the ground, he went to the place of the blanket. When his navel itched, he could not reach it, so he scratched it with a fire shovel. (S. Ahmad). in the next passage, the writer managed to create a comic effect by exaggerating the portrait of the hero: "In our area there lived a giant named Mamajon Lomboz. He was not very tall, but if he was a quarter of an inch wide, he was over two feet. When he sat down, his buttocks swelled like a cake and formed a three-gas circle. His stomach was so sagging that when he sat down on the ground, he went to the place of the blanket. When his navel itched, he could not reach it, so he scratched it with a fire shovel. (S. Ahmad). When his navel itched, he could not reach it, so he scratched it with a fire shovel. (S. Ahmad). When his navel itched, he could not reach it, so he scratched it with a fire shovel. (S. Ahmad). He was not very tall, but if he was a quarter of an inch wide, he was over two feet. When he sat down, his buttocks swelled like a cake and formed a three-gas circle. His stomach was so sagging that when he sat down on the ground, he went to the place of the blanket. When his navel itched, he could not reach it, so he scratched it with a fire shovel. (S. Ahmad). When his navel itched, he could not reach it, so he scratched it with a fire shovel. (S. Ahmad). When his navel itched, he could not reach it, so he scratched it with a fire shovel. (S. Ahmad). He was not very tall, but if he was a quarter of an inch wide, he was over two feet. When he sat down, his buttocks swelled like a cake and formed a three-gas circle. His stomach was so sagging that when he sat down on the ground, he went to the place of the blanket. When his navel itched, he could not reach it, so he scratched it with a fire shovel. (S. Ahmad). When his navel itched, he could not reach it, so he scratched it with a fire shovel. (S. Ahmad). When his navel itched, he could not reach it, so he scratched it with a fire shovel. (S. Ahmad). When his navel itched, he could not reach it, so he scratched it with a fire shovel. (S. Ahmad). When his navel itched, he could not reach it, so he scratched it with a fire shovel. (S. Ahmad). When his navel itched, he could not reach it, so he scratched it with a fire shovel. (S. Ahmad). When his navel itched, he could not reach it, so he scratched it with a fire shovel. (S. Ahmad). When his navel itched, he could not reach it, so he scratched it with a fire shovel. (S. Ahmad). When his navel itched, he could not reach it, so he scratched it with a fire shovel. (S. Ahmad).

Another way of creating comic effect through exaggeration is called grotesque. Grotesque is a French word meaning absurd, unnatural. Grotesque satire is a frightening and comic exaggeration of reality by mixing fantasy with it. The grotesque does not deny reality, but is the art of expressing reality more spectacularly in realistic, unnatural forms. In most feuilletons of Abdullah Kahkhor, negative situations, social and spiritual vices that occur in marriage are grotesquely revealed. The writer's feuilleton called "Bildirish" tells about "Cholok Doml", who made a profession of flattering people, calling himself a healer and doctor. The patients he treats, the medicines he recommends, and the way he works are put in an unnatural way: Patients he treats: Women with swollen breasts, women who do not give birth, women suffering from love pain, madmen, fairies, brides who have thrown away their burdens. Especially for those who are haunted by chazanrezzes, jinn and ghosts that recur during menstruation, etc. Examples of medicines: Mushroom leaf, oil in the air, then soot from a pipe, water from a pipe, a rattle from a pipe basket and In addition, there are various drugs that are not in the lawyer's box. Our last two experiments to fix jinn will be on jinn with grain in the Mirtohir region of Kokan. For Tashra, eight shovels and seven hoes are prescribed. The most suitable for medicine is the skin of the stomach of Khamrokulov. brides who have shed their burdens. Especially for those who are haunted by chazanrezzes, jinn and ghosts that recur during menstruation, etc. Examples of medicines: Mushroom leaf, oil in the air, then soot from a pipe, water from a pipe, rattle from the pipe basket and In addition, there are various drugs that are not in the lawyer's box. Our last two experiments to fix jinn will be on jinn with grain in the Mirtohir region of Kokan. For Tashra, eight shovels and seven hoes are prescribed. The most suitable for medicine is the skin of the stomach of Khamrokulov. brides who have shed their burdens. Especially for those who are haunted by chazanrezzes, jinn and ghosts that recur during menstruation, etc. Examples of medicines: Mushroom leaf, oil in the air, then soot from a pipe, water from a pipe, a rattle from a pipe basket and In addition, there are various drugs that are not in the lawyer's box. Our last two experiments to fix jinn will be on jinn with grain in the Mirtohir region of Kokan. For Tashra, eight shovels and seven hoes are prescribed. The most suitable for medicine is the skin of the stomach of Khamrokulov. the rumble of a cart and various medicines that are not in the clerk's box. Our last two experiments to fix jinn will be on jinn with grain in the Mirtohir region of Kokan. For Tashra, eight shovels and seven hoes are prescribed. The most suitable for medicine is the skin of the stomach of Khamrokulov. the rumble of a cart and various medicines that are not in the clerk's box. Our last two experiments to fix jinn will be on jinn with grain in the Mirtohir region of Kokan. For Tashra, eight shovels and seven hoes are prescribed. The most suitable for medicine is the skin of the stomach of Khamrokulov. the rumble of a cart and various medicines that are not in the clerk's box. Our last two experiments to fix jinn will be on jinn with grain in the Mirtohir region of Kokan. For Tashra, eight shovels and seven hoes are prescribed. The most suitable for medicine is the skin of the stomach of Khamrokulov. the rumble of a cart and various medicines that are not in the clerk's box. Our last two experiments to fix jinn will be on jinn with grain in the Mirtohir region of Kokan. For Tashra, eight shovels and seven hoes are prescribed. The most suitable for medicine is the skin of the stomach of Khamrokulov.

Decrease (litot) means the opposite of exaggeration. But in essence they are not opposite phenomena, both of them serve to describe reality by exaggerating it, only there is a difference in the way of expression: in hyperbole, reality is directly exaggerated. means of reducing reality. - Don't bite my tongue, cock! Didn't I tell you that in autumn you will crawl under the table... Well, you still have fourteen percent to become a rooster (A. Kahhor). Belittling another person as a "cockerel" emphasizes that he is strong. Or, if the first speaker in the example below uses an exaggeration, the speech of the second speaker is both an understatement and an exaggeration.

One tall man came to the house of another tall man and said:

- I brought you a carpet as a gift, one of its ends is here, and the other end is in Samarkand.

The second attic immediately answered him:

- Thank you, you did a good job, a small section of the carpet caught fire in the hotel, I will patch up the carpet that you gave me.

QUESTIONS AND TASKS:

1. For what purposes is a metaphor used in a literary text?
2. For what purpose is metonymy used in a literary text?
3. What is the purpose of synecdoche in a literary text?
4. What are the goals of using irony in a literary text?
5. For what purposes is the paraphrase used in a literary text?
6. What are the goals of exaggeration in a literary text?
7. For what purposes is the grotesque used in a literary text?
8. What is the purpose of diminution in a literary text?

LECTURE 8
PRINCIPLES OF TEXT ANALYSIS IN DIFFERENT STYLES.
2 hours.

This topic provides detailed information about the methodology, method, principle, method, the principle of unity of form and content, the principle of unity of space and time, the method of scientific observation, the method of language transformation, the method of comparing text options, methods of reasoning in dictionaries.

Plan:

1. Principles of literary text analysis.
2. Types of linguistic analysis
3. Methods of analysis of journalistic and scientific texts.

Educational literature:

1. Abdurakhmanov Kh., Makhmudov N. Aesthetics of the word. - Tashkent: Teacher, 2002.

2. Boboev T., Boboeva Z. Visual arts. - Tashkent: TDPU, 2001.

3. M. Yuldoshev, M. Isakov, Sh. Geydarov. Linguistic analysis of a literary text. - Tashkent: Publishing House of the National Library of Uzbekistan. A. Navoi, 2010.

4. Yuldoshev B. Fundamentals of phraseological methodology. - Samarkand, 1999.

5. Yuldoshev M. Linguo-poetics of a literary text. - Tashkent: Science, 2008.

6. Yuldoshev M., Yadgarov K. Organization of practical classes on linguistic analysis of a literary text. - Tashkent: TDPU them. Nizomi, 2007.

7. Yuldoshev M. Secrets of the word "Cholpon". - Tashkent: Spirituality, 2002.

8. Mamadzhanov A. Linguistics of the text. - Tashkent, 1999.

9. Meliev S. Dynamics of the word in the context // Uzbek language and literature, 1983. - No. 4.-B. 50-54.

10. Umirkulov B. Lexicon of poetic speech. - Tashkent: Science, 1990.

The methodology of science "Philological analysis of the text" is based on the laws of dialectical thinking. The word "methodology" comes from the Greek words "methodos" - the way, method, and "logos" - teaching. In other words, this is the doctrine of the correct organization and organization of the theoretical and practical activities of a person. Dialectical thinking reveals the essence of things and events, their relationship and development with the help of philosophical laws, concepts (categories). The laws and concepts of dialectics reflect the most general relations between things and events in reality and create an opportunity for a person to delve into the essence of things and consciously analyze them. But when these laws are applied to a particular work of art, it is necessary to take into account its specificity.

We believe that in the process of linguistic analysis of a literary text, it would be advisable to work on the basis of the following principles:

1. The principle of unity of form and content.

2. The principle of the unity of space and time.

3. The principle of determining the relationship of the language of a literary text to the national language and literary language.

4. Principles for identifying poetic actualized language means in a literary text.

5. The principle of determining the mechanisms of intertextuality in a literary text.

The following are recognized as analytical methods:

1. Linguistic method.

2. Method for comparing text options.

3. Method based on dictionaries.

4. Methodology for compiling an index of language units.

1. The principle of unity of form and content. One of the types of connection between things and events in being is the dialectic of form and content. The concept of the dialectical unity of form and content is a necessary feature of any text. Philosophers evaluate the content as "a set of internal elements and changes that characterize certain things and events." They interpret form as "a way of expressing content, an organizer." Form and content are so intertwined that the apparent defect of one can undermine the integrity of the other. If the harmony of form and content is violated, the author's intention will not be fully disclosed. By focusing on the balance between the text and its genre,

A literary text is a complex and multi-layered aesthetic whole, completely unique both in form and content. In it, the content is as important as the form. Sometimes form can even rise to the level of content, take on the status of content, and affect the value of the actual content. Of particular importance in art is the ability of the author to formulate content and individual characteristics. In a linguo-poetic analysis of a literary text, this side, i.e., the unity of form and content, should be considered first of all as the primary principle. Open or hidden compatibility of form and content is a serious basis for a clear and complete manifestation of the author's artistic intent.

2. The principle of the unity of space and time. When considering the linguistic features of a literary text, it is necessary to approach each event in it, taking into account the concept of the unity of space and time. Any work occurs in relation to space and time. The language of a work on a historical theme includes lexical and grammatical units that specify in what place and in what environment events take place that carry the spirit of a certain time. The concept of space and time is not unique to a work of art. This applies to any text view. When conducting an analysis according to this principle, one of the diachronic and synchronic aspects should be chosen depending on the period of writing the text, the topic raised in the text, the nature of the text units. We will consider this on the basis of the following passage from the story of the great artist of the word Abdullah Kahhor:

"Yes, did you lose your cow?"

- No... it wasn't a cow, it was an ox.

Did he exist before he disappeared? What was this bull?

- Olya bull...

- Was it a good bull or a bad bull?

- Double Room...

- Can a good ox walk if someone leads it?

There is nothing in my bios...

- You won't come back yourself? Why is he crying? A? Do not Cry!(Selected works. T. 1. S. 33).

Where, at what time and among what people this conversation takes place, you can find out from this short passage. The question is short, as is the answer. In the manner of asking questions, one feels arrogance, contempt, a careless attitude to reality, as if looking at something worthless. The tone of pitching, swearing and ridicule is clearly reflected. The answer shows the simplicity and poverty of the hero. The conversation takes place in the presence of Amin. Accordingly, formal speech elements were used.

When considering the linguistic and poetic features of a literary text, it is necessary to approach each linguistic event in it with the concept of the unity of space and time. Because any work is created in time and space.

3. The principle of determining the relationship between the literary language and the national language of a literary text. Another principle is to consider the relationship of the language of the analyzed text to the national language and literary language. As V. V. Vinogradov argued in his work "On the Language of Fiction" (1959), the historical movement of the language of fiction cannot be studied in isolation from the history of the national language and its various branches. Two types of literary text can be distinguished: 1) modern text (created today) 2) historical text (created in the past). In turn, two types of modern text can be observed, namely: a) a modern text on today's topic, b) a modern text on a historical topic. For example, S. Ahmad's story "Azrael passed the roads" is a modern text of today's season, "Ulug Sultanat" by M. Ali is a modern text, "Farhad and Shirin" by Navoi is a historical text.

4. The principle of identifying poetically actualized language means in a literary text. The definition of poetic actualized language means in a work of art is also one of the important principles. Having revealed the linguistic and artistic essence of such means, one can clearly imagine the mechanisms for the formation and expression of artistic content.

5. The principle of determining the linguo-semantic features of the mechanisms of intertextuality in a literary text. Alternate text used within text

identify its forms (such as an example, imitation, narration, hadith, narration, myths, legends, didactems, a work or fragment of a particular creator) and how compatible they are with the content of the work, their place in expressing artistic content, with the main text understanding important situations in the linguistic and semantic connection is extremely necessary when revealing the linguopoetics of a literary text.

1. Linguistic conversion method. Tabdil- means to replace, change, replace. Some literature says that it is also used in relation to the use of related words in pairs. The results of this method of analysis are used to determine the artistry of the language of the work, the plausibility, the authorship of the writer. It is intended for restructuring words or phrases, sentences used in the work, replacing them with similar ones and grading on this basis. For example, pay attention to such an example from the story "Pomegranate" by Abdullah Kahhor: "With your power, he will not say a word!" said Turobzhan, tickling the brought rag, chew it!

Here the word "fabric" is deliberately used, and not the word "thing". The word thing is stylistically neutral, and the word fabric is semantically neutral, that is, it has a facet of meaning associated with distinction. In the eyes of a woman who is obsessed with pomegranates and expects her husband to bring pomegranates, the bee's nest is waxy honey, and the pure honey itself is nothing but cloth. The general intonation of the story, the development of the story does not allow replacing the word fabric with another synonym. Such cases can be found in the works of the skilled writer Cholpon.

For example, in the Uzbek language there are a number of words with the same meaning as "oramak", "burkamak", "chulgamag", "chirmamak" and the word "burkamak". ' has many more "wrap" features than the word "oramaq". that is, in its semantic construction there is an additional scheme of the expression "leave no free space". Therefore, in this passage, Cholpon increased the accuracy and expressiveness of the image, choosing to express the corresponding content not the word cape, but the word burkamak: the long hem of the veil filled her armpits like a big knot. That is why the units in this place cannot be replaced by synonyms or any other word. rather, by choosing the word burkamak, they achieved an increase in accuracy and expressiveness in the image: This little girl, not yet included in the ranks of a well-dressed person, was wrapped in a cloak of older women, and a long burqa skirt filled her armpits like a big knot. That is why the units in this place cannot be replaced by synonyms or any other word. rather, by choosing the word burkamak, they achieved an increase in accuracy and expressiveness in the image: This little girl, who has not yet entered the ranks of a well-dressed person, was wrapped in a cloak of older women, and a long burqa skirt filled her armpits like a big knot. That is why the units in this place cannot be replaced by synonyms or any other word.

2. Method for comparing text options. Using this method, the text of a certain work is compared with other versions, and the essence of linguistic differences is explained in relation to the author's point of view, the artistic and aesthetic design and idea of the work. This method works well in studying the work of a writer on the language of a literary work, in identifying various means of author's corrections aimed at expressing the same content, and in general in determining the writer's skill in using language. For example, in the manuscript of the novel Navoi: "Grandma," Dildar said excitedly, "if you see him, tell him that he has no bad intentions, let him go quietly" (p. 600). In the publication: - Grandmother, - he whispered, - if you see him, tell him he has no bad intentions, let him go quietly (p. 237). In this episode, the conversation takes place near the gates of the royal harem. The combination of situation and mental state is clearly seen in the second variant. Or the hero of Gafur Ghulam's work "Shum bola" - Karavoy in the first edition is given 17, and in the next - 14. Here, too, the compatibility of the character's behavior with age was taken into account. These are direct copyright corrections. There are cases when the text of a work is deliberately changed by publishers or literary critics. Many people know that the novel "Otkan Kunlar" was published with some changes. the text of the work is deliberately changed by publishers or literary critics. Many people know that the novel "Otkan Kunlar" was published with some changes. the text of the work is deliberately changed by publishers or literary critics. Many people know that the novel "Otkan Kunlar" was published with some changes. The combination of situation and mental state is clearly seen in the second variant. Or the hero of Gafur Ghulam's work "Shum bola" - Karavoy in the first edition is given 17, and in the next - 14. Here, too, the compatibility of the character's behavior with age was taken into account. These are direct copyright corrections. There are cases when the text of a work is deliberately changed by publishers or literary critics. Many people know that the novel "Otkan Kunlar" was published with some changes. the text of the work is deliberately changed by publishers or literary critics. Many people know that the novel "Otkan Kunlar" was published with some changes. the text of the work is deliberately changed by publishers or literary critics. Many people know that the novel "Otkan Kunlar" was published with some changes. The combination of situation and mental state is clearly seen in the second variant. Or the hero of Gafur Ghulam's work "Shum bola" - Karavoy in the first edition is given 17, and in the next - 14. Here, too, the compatibility of the character's behavior with age was taken into account. These are direct copyright corrections. There are cases when the text of a work is deliberately changed by publishers or literary critics. Many people know that the novel "Otkan Kunlar" was published with some changes. the text of the work is deliberately changed by publishers or literary critics. Many people know that the novel "Otkan Kunlar" was published with some changes. the text of the work is deliberately changed by publishers or literary critics. Many people know that the novel "Otkan Kunlar" was published with some changes. Or the hero of Gafur Ghulam's work "Shum bola" - Karavoy in the first edition is given 17, and in the next - 14. Here, too, the compatibility of the character's behavior with age was taken into account. These are direct copyright corrections. There are cases when the text of a work is deliberately changed by publishers or literary critics. Many people know that the novel "Otkan Kunlar" was published with some changes. the text of the work is deliberately changed by publishers or literary critics. Many people know that the novel "Otkan Kunlar" was published with some changes. the text of the work is deliberately changed by publishers or literary critics. Many people know that the novel "Otkan Kunlar" was published with some changes. Or the hero of Gafur Ghulam's work "Shum bola" - Karavoy in the first edition is given 17, and in the next - 14. Here, too, the compatibility of the character's behavior with age was taken into account. These are direct copyright corrections. There are cases when the text of a work is deliberately changed by publishers or literary critics. Many people know that the novel "Otkan Kunlar" was published with some changes. the text of the work is deliberately changed by publishers or literary critics. Many people know that the novel "Otkan Kunlar" was published with some changes. the text of the work is deliberately changed by publishers or literary critics. Many people know that the novel "Otkan Kunlar" was published with some changes. when the text of a work is intentionally changed by publishers or literary critics. Many people know that the novel "Otkan Kunlar" was published with some changes. the text of the work is deliberately changed by publishers or literary critics. Many people know that the novel "Otkan Kunlar" was published with some changes. the text of the work is deliberately changed by publishers or literary critics. Many people know that the novel "Otkan Kunlar" was published with some changes. when the text of a work is intentionally changed by publishers or literary critics. Many people know that the novel "Otkan Kunlar" was published with some changes. the text of the work is deliberately changed by publishers or literary critics. Many people know that the novel "Otkan Kunlar" was published with some changes. the text of the work is deliberately changed by publishers or literary critics. Many people know that the novel "Otkan Kunlar" was published with some changes.

3. Method based on dictionaries. The language of the work, especially the linguistic features of works or translated works on historical subjects, should be referred to the appropriate dictionaries. For example, knowledge of the meaning of such military terms as gudar, savash, sovut, sadok, hum, tuv, bayadok, used in the language of the Shaibani Khan epic, helps to carefully study the work. Since this work is several hundred years old, it becomes simply necessary to create a dictionary for works written at the beginning of the last century. For example, dictionaries of the works of such poets and writers as Mukimi, Furkat, Zavki, Avaz O'tar, Abdulla Kadiri, Abdurauf Fitrat, Abdulhamid Suleiman oglu Cholpon should be compiled based on the meanings of special words implemented in the work. In Otkan Kunlar, under each page, there is an explanation of some obscure words. For example, utta—there; Siporish - appointment: kodukuttab - suitable, suitable; ashraf - noble people, grandees; consultant - consultant; The interviewer is like an interlocutor. And this is not only in this work, but also in others. But it is necessary to prepare a special dictionary dedicated to the language of all the works of the writer.

Zh. Lapasov's manual "Fictional text and linguistic analysis" contains examples of creating a dictionary of a specific literary text and important instructions for working with the dictionary. As the scientist rightly noted, "Linguistic analysis of a literary text is difficult to imagine without various dictionaries. Working with a dictionary is one of the most important factors in the development of vocabulary, oral and written speech of schoolchildren and students, and with the help of this dictionary, not only the basic meanings of words are revealed, but also the meanings of hma, the linguistic element of each word, its etymology (history of origin and gradual development words), its structure and sometimes its grammatical form are well known.

4. Methodology for compiling an index of language units. When analyzing a literary text, it is required to create an index of a language unit in a work. To do this, first determine the most used units in the work, characteristic of the work of art (for example, there may be phrases, synonyms, antonyms or combinations of epithets, metonymy, metaphors). It is then sorted alphabetically. It serves as factual material to highlight the language skills of the writer. For example, we can compile an index of more than a hundred phrases, metaphors or metonyms used in the novel by the master of the word Abdulla Kahkhor "Sarob" as follows: (5 volumes. Volume 1. Literature named after Gafur Gulom, Tashkent, and art publishing house, 1987).

Phrases:

To distort the image "If I move, my ass burns", Saidi said, wrinkling his face as if it was now stinging. (p. 41).

Take it around your neck- Saidi said goodbye and took the liberty to go to the village. (p. 83).

fall into the air- *Kendzha, when Saidy Yakubjon said **got into it**.* (p. 124).

Deliver without drops- *When he arrived in Sozor, they said that he saw signs of intelligence in Saidi, that this young man was above ordinary students, and that*

Munis Khan would deliver Sayidi without a drop of water. (p. 67).

To open up the sky- *When he arrived in the village, at first it was very difficult for him to get used to the new environment, but after he got used to it, he got used to it.* (p. 89).

Don't let your heart beat- *Munish Khan turned up the collar of his coat and froze, not wanting to go out the door.* (p. 43).

Not able to make it- *Can't you work with a cook?* (p. 82).

Listen- *The girl listened to his words as if listening to a sentence pronounced on her.* (page 35).

Metaphors:

Shervaccha *"Hello, my dear," said the old voice, and the owner of that voice was greeted with a "thump."* (p. 88) - *Shervaccia,- said the old man, putting both hands on his chest and groaning, - if they give the newspaper ...* (p. 89).

Threads of proximity *Little by little, the bonds of intimacy that Ehsan had created between them began to break. (p. 42).*

Tongak - *This conversation between "Tongak" and the professor shocked the entire university. (p. 43).*

Metonymy:

Hall - Another explosion of applause seemed to shake the hall. (p. 94). The whole hall looked at the teacher (p. 94).

Big small - He said that in order to write "big", you must first attract readers "small". (p. 136).

lovers - In particular, "Lovers" by Kenji Saidi was an open attack on the policy of the Shura government regarding the freedom of women, (...) Abbas Khan himself needed to be consoled. (p. 139).

Faculty - If you feel such a desire to leave the faculty, do not reluctantly continue, because this will lead to expulsion from the faculty. (p. 106).

Sect "Then, of course, we will follow the path indicated by the sect." (p. 94).

University - *The university is calling.* (p. 91) Professor with "Tongak".

The entire university was shocked by this conversation. (p. 43).

Glass - *The more glass, the easier.* (p. 112).

Types of linguistic analysis. As there are principles and methods for analyzing a literary text, so there are specific types. The purpose, direction and scope of the analysis can be divided into two, given the scope of work: thematic and complex analysis.

1. Thematic analysis. It is designed to analyze a work of art on one aspect of the language and on certain principles and methods. Thematic analysis is mainly carried out at one of the language levels. For example, let's say we analyze Cholpon's novel "Night and Kunduz" from a lexico-semantic point of view. Lexical units in the work are distinguished (some words, phrases, proverbs, sayings, aphorisms). It is determined to what extent lexical units serve the art of the work, whether they are traditional or individual. Methods of connecting text components are studied separately. The types of texts and their features are considered.

2. Complex analysis. The complex analysis is based on the study of language units characteristic of all areas, and their use in a particular work in relation to the general content, genre and structural structure of the text. This type of analysis acquires a general philological orientation, content and character. Therefore, before analyzing the text, we must know the basic laws of the areas related to literary criticism and linguistics. A comprehensive analysis will be dedicated to a specific artist. Such an analysis can be carried out for one work at different levels or for several works at the same level. For example, the linguopoetics of Abdulla Kadiri's novel "O'tkan kunlar" (according to language levels). Or the linguopoetics of the works of Abdulla Kadiri. At the same time, the linguistic features of all the works of the writer are checked, the results are summarized and analyzed. This is not an easy task. And it's not the work of one or two people. A comprehensive study and analysis of literary works, the collection of all the work done so far, the creation of a database with a classification index, the preparation of the necessary dictionaries and other works are included in the field of linguopoetics, which is developing rapidly. .

QUESTIONS AND TASKS:

1. What do you understand by methodology, method, principle and method?

2. How is the principle of unity of form and content used in the process of analyzing a literary text?

3. What do you understand by the principle of the unity of space and time?

4. How would you explain the principle of determining the relation of the language of a literary text to the national language and literary language?

5. What do you understand by the principle of identifying poetically actualized language means in a literary text?

6. How do you understand the principle of determining the linguistic and semantic features of the mechanisms of intertextuality in a literary text?

7. What methods are used in the analysis of a literary text?

8. What types of linguistic analysis do you know?

Linguistic analysis of journalistic and popular science texts. Human organs and other related phenomena may later trigger migration. For example, the eye first began to represent the human organ of vision, and then other similar objects found in nature. The eye of a ring, the eye of a needle, the eye of a spring, etc. Prior to this study in the Uzbek language, devoted to the study of anthropomorphism, scientific texts were practically not analyzed. Recognized mainly in literary texts. In order to fully identify anthropomorphic metaphors and their specific features, it is necessary to analyze texts of different styles from linguistic, sociolinguistic and linguoculturological points of view. Also, learning to use comparative anthropomorphic metaphors will allow you to better understand it.

anthropomorphic metaphor. This is a metaphor created on the basis of a person's name and objects belonging to him (body part, clothes), and is a metaphorical transfer of the meaning of such lexemes as foot, hand, mouth, tongue, tooth, ear, neck, collar.[113].

Yu.M.Aleksandrova, Yu.V.Gorshunov emphasize that a unique feature of the works of J.Darrell is the ability to give a vivid description of animals, using the features of the image of people by comparing the animal world with human society. The comparison is based on the natural color of the animal, which is the same or similar to work clothes or habits similar to the usual actions of people of any profession or social status.[114]. If this is an example of the expression of anthropomorphic metaphors in literary texts, then it is necessary to form certain ideas about how metaphors are used in other speech situations, including journalistic speeches.

Metaphor is used in various functional forms of speech. The study studies the linguistic, sociolinguistic and cognitive features of metaphors in literary texts. In fact, anthropomorphic metaphors are effectively used in journalistic, even scientific and official styles of speech. For example, when studying anthropomorphic metaphors in the headlines of Russian and American newspapers, the most developed model of conceptual vectors of anxiety, aggression, deviation from the natural order of things (illness, etc.) is revealed. In particular, E. S. Abramova in Russian linguistics[115]anthropomorphic metaphors emphasize that the discourse of modern Russian media reflects the path of social changes, spiritual, moral and ideological quests that have taken place in Russian society for many years.

---

[113]Khohamkulov A. On the classification of metaphor in the Uzbek language. Collection of scientific articles dedicated to the 20th anniversary of the independence of the Republic of Uzbekistan. Linguist. 2 books. – T.: Akademnashr, 2011. – B. 85–88.

[114]Yu.M. Aleksandrova, Yu.V. Gorshunov Anthropomorphic metaphors reflecting the professional and social specificity of a person // Humanitarian Sciences Series. 2017. S-22

[115]http://www.rusnauka.com/17_PMN_2014/Philologia/9_172101.doc.htm

Media discourse is also understood as a socially preferred principle of understanding and interpreting socially significant meanings in the media, as well as a social regulatory mechanism that controls public consciousness by creating and reproducing socially significant meanings and assessments in the media.

This study is focused on understanding the movement of dominant meanings and their linguistic nature in the context of changes in public consciousness under the influence of internal and external factors in the process of comprehending the cultural space of Russian society.[116]

In the modern socio-cultural context, the newspapers "Jamiyat" and "Marifat" are of particular importance as serious, intellectual and authoritative scientific and educational periodicals aimed at comprehending the cultural, spiritual and moral foundations of society, its present day and its role in the history of human civilization.

Journalists and bloggers in the Uzbek media use metaphors so that their ideas are quickly understood by readers and have an effective impact. The use of anthropomorphic metaphors is especially common in newspaper headlines. For example, "Today's conversation: the press lives" in the newspaper "Jamiat".[117](Society, November 26, 2020) - article under the title. In this case, the verb "to live" has, of course, a figurative meaning, taken in relation to a person. The first sentence of the article uses the metaphor: "I think a lot about the power and influence of the press." The word "power" in this sentence, of course, goes back to the meaning of spiritual power in a person.

---

[116]Yu.M. Aleksandrova, Yu.V. Gorshunov Anthropomorphic metaphors reflecting the professional and social specificity of a person // Humanitarian Sciences Series. 2017. S-23
[117]https://www.bong.uz/zhamiyat/1373-1373

Again, the same article uses the metaphorical meaning of "to die" as opposed to the verb to live. It is true that death is not unique to Jesus, but the lexeme used in the following sentence represents a biological phenomenon characteristic of humans, which can be classified as an anthropomorphic metaphor: in anticipation, President Shavkat Mirziyoyev, in his address to teachers and intellectuals in September on December 30 of this years emphasized the importance and role of newspapers, and we were very happy about this."

"Are Regional Information Resource Centers Ogyi?"[118] the named article also acquires a metaphorical meaning, this figurative word initially expresses a characteristic characteristic of people, but it can be seen that it creates an anthropomorphic metaphor in the language of the media.

Such analyzes should be carried out on journalistic texts on a wider scale, since when studying metaphors only on the basis of literary texts, one can come to a one-sided conclusion, and studying their use in scientific and even official texts allows one to fully reveal the sociolinguistic essence of anthropomorphic metaphors. As a result of scientific ideas about the figurative meanings of words, the scope of the use of metaphors is expanding.

Linguistic and cultural features of metaphors in scientific texts. The scientific study of metaphor began with Aristotle and was continued by his followers in his writings. A. Richards, M. Black, N. D. Arutyunova, M. Johnson, J. Lakoff and other well-known linguists continued to study metaphor and had a great influence on determining its place and role in language, on debunking scientific ideas on this subject. Due to the fact that the anthropocentric approach to language occupies a major place in modern linguistics,

---
[118] https://bit.ly/3lmXPnG

much attention is paid to the study of anthropomorphic metaphors in relation to various speech situations. Since metaphors have brightness, imagery, expressiveness and emotionality, one of the main tasks of speech is to achieve impact, and not to convey information.

In world linguistics, more and more attention is paid to the study of anthropomorphic metaphors in scientific and official texts. In particular, Russian linguists have studied this issue in detail in their research. A. V. Myasnikova[119], Arutyunova N.D.[120], many linguists, such as S. G. Dudetskaya, I. V. Pashkova, E. E. Pimenova and N. O. Samarkina, emphasize that anthropomorphic metaphors play an important role in explaining complex concepts, describing the environment, thinking processes and perception.

Sevinj Maharramova metaphor is based on comparison, a person can compare the unknown with the known, and this shows his attitude to objective reality. Since time immemorial, metaphorization has been applied primarily to words denoting the most familiar concepts and objects from the immediate environment of a person.[121] it says that.

Ya. A. Arzhanova[122] In his article, he focuses on the functions of anthropomorphic metaphor in the English-language economic discourse. He argues that anthropomorphic metaphors are being explored as stylistically effective devices in modern English economic texts. From this point of view, the analysis of communicative-functional anthropomorphic metaphors in scientific and economic texts to a certain extent expands the list of tasks of anthropomorphic

---

[119] https://lektsii.org/12-47199.html

[120] Arutyunova, N.D. Metaphor and discourse / N.D. Arutyunova // Theory of metaphor / General. ed. N.D. Arutyunova, M.A. Yurinskiy. - M.: Progress, 1990. - S. 5-32.

[121] https://gisap.eu/ru/node/7709
[122] https://cyberleninka.ru/article/n/funktsii-antropomorfnoy-metafory-v-angloyazychnom-ekonomicheskom-diskurse/viewer

metaphors and shows how important their descriptive and expressive potential is even in a journalistic text.

Economic concepts, as well as concepts related to other areas of human activity, can be expressed by various visual means. The most popular and productive stylistic unit here is the metaphor. Thanks to metaphor, simple and complex economic phenomena can be clearly and figuratively described. The presence of a metaphor in the text allows the recipient to understand that the author puts something else into the word, not related to its literal meaning.

In this regard, I.A. Arzhanova suggests the following strategy for the receiver to describe what the speaker means:

1) the recipient's awareness that this statement is not verbatim and that its misinterpretation may disrupt successful communication;

2) the recipient is trying to associate the metaphor with a number of object variants;

3) the recipient finds among the possible values the one that best suits the given context and situation.[123]

The analysis shows that the anthropomorphic metaphor is complexly structured and has a high pragmatic potential. His model consists of the frames "body", "parts of the body", "appearance", "human character".

The use of metaphors is also very effective in medical scientific discourse. It uses metaphors to refer to diseases to be treated, the signs and symptoms of diseases, and their consequences. The use of metaphors in popular science speech also gives positive results.

The use of metaphors in the field of energy allows you to express thoughts clearly and understandably. In such texts, meanings are

---

[123] Arzhanova I.A. Functional approach and interrogative training in adequate metaphorical and theoretical-practical translation // Integration of education. 2013. No. 2. S. 136-142.

conveyed on the basis of the similarity of individual signs, movements, and forms. "Heat engines use gases, vapor-gas mixtures or water vapor as working fluids, since the working fluids must have the properties of expansion and compression. For example, in internal combustion engines, air is the working fluid, it receives thermal energy generated during the combustion of fuel, and performs mechanical work, pushing the piston in the process of expansion.[124]

Or in texts on geometry, human behavior is transferred to objects, inanimate objects:

If each point of a given form F in space is somehow shifted, then a new figure F1 is formed. If during this transfer (reflection) different points of the first form move to different points of the second form, then such a transfer is called a geometric shift of the form.

Permutation of similarity in space reflects a straight line into a straight line, a ray into a ray, a cross section into a cross section and an angle into an angle. Also, this permutation will reflect plane to plane.[125]

The highlighted words have different meanings in the context.

In the theory of linguistics, metaphorical words are used to explain the nature of linguistic phenomena and their understandable expression. For example, when studying the field of phonetics, there is a need for a figurative explanation of the processes associated with sounds. For example"...abbreviations (absorption of phonemes) are based on..."[126] The highlighted word in this sentence has a metaphorical meaning. In the sentence "the rate of absorption of ions

---

[124] Khudoyberdiev T.S. and others. Textbook for heat engineering and basic universities. - Tashkent. 2008 Cholpon Publishing House

[125] BK Khaidarov. Geometry, part I, textbook for students of grade 11 of general educational institutions and secondary specialized, vocational educational institutions, 1 edition, Press and Information Agency of Uzbekistan "Uzbekistan" publishing house, house of creativity 2017.

[126] Eltazarov J. The principle of economy and reduction in language. Monograph. - Samarkand: SamDU, 2004. S. 29.

depends on their number in the medium" there is another figurative meaning, different from the absorption of sound.

The active expression of anthropomorphic metaphors in scientific texts is also shown in the following example:*"No other method can compete with chromatography, a method of physical and chemical research, in its versatility and efficiency in the separation of complex mixtures."*[127] The inability to compete is actually a characteristic of human behavior. The application of its scientific language to substances leads to a clear, figurative, understandable expression of thought.

In general, the speaker took advantage of this, realizing that anthropomorphic metaphors are an active language tool in society, and that they can make any communication on various topics carried out by members of the society effective and productive. The study of linguistic, stylistic, socio-pragmatic and pragmatic functions of anthropomorphic metaphors in scientific texts serves the development of scientific language. In Uzbek linguistics, special attention should be paid to the study of metaphors in a scientific context.

Anthropomorphic metaphors are also used in scientific texts. This type of text is characterized by the presence of commonly used scientific terms, and often the author uses various metaphors to help the readerit was easier to understand this or that term. In our study, this is expressed through the analysis of anthropomorphic metaphors. For example, energy can drop very quickly and suddenly at any moment, because no one can predict the behavior of the weather, this is what the author uses. An anthropomorphic metaphor: UK electricity prices have skyrocketed. Lack of energy worries everyone. When a metaphorical word enters the text, it

---

[127]Mukhamadiev N.K. Physical and chemical bases of optimization and identification of the separation process in chromatography Bulletin of SamGU. Samarkand, 2017. 152 pages.

increases interest and usually embellishes speech emotionally. As you can see, the use of anthropomorphic metaphors is very common in non-fiction texts. The use of such techniques in popular science texts not only simplifies it, but also makes the content of the text understandable and interesting for the reader, attracting attention. The use of anthropomorphic metaphors helps the reader to understand the concepts of "energy", "economics",

Metaphor - a word or expression used in a figurative sense, is a meaning based on an anonymous comparison of an object with another object on the basis of a common feature. Thus, it is important to make a textual comparison of the most common methods used in one popular science text. A scientific term by analogy: "Today, celestial bodies claim their role. In such scientific texts, comparisons and analogies are often used: "the birth of the Universe", "black holes absorb everything", "the reactor breathes". Also, the personification of the depicted objects is a real human image: "the universe is the mother." Metaphor makes it possible to use comparisons and comparisons in popular science texts to popularize the truth about complex modern phenomena. For example,

Metaphor is a universal phenomenon. Its main task is to help you understand abstract things more easily.

A.P. According to Chudinov, "metaphors in the texts under consideration are often not a random set of completely autonomous elements, but extra-textual signs in the same mechanism, characterized by a strong textual and strong system.[128]. Metaphorical

---

[128]Chudinov, A.P. Russia in the metaphorical mirror: a cognitive study of political metaphor: a study guide / A.P. Chudinov. - Yekaterinburg: Publishing House of the Ural State Pedagogical University, 2001. - 238 p.

model in popular science texts by A.P. Chudinov identified the following features of the metaphorical model:

1. Initial conceptual field (initial field) - a model of field units, which are conceptually embraced non-figurative values.

2. New conceptual space (target space) - units containing the metaphorical meanings of the corresponding models for the conceptual space.

3. The model is associated with frames, each of which is understood as part of a simple language picture of the world.

4. Standard nests that make up each frame, that is, situations where the elements make up some part of the frame, some of its specific features.

5. The productivity of the placement model and the possibility of modeling placement areas in the text. You can also calculate the frequency. Using the appropriate metaphor models, frequency comparison allows you to create texts of different models, taking into account stylistic, genre and other features. The definition of this metaphorical model lies in the fact that conceptual relations are the basis for modeling a conceptual system, which is a system of frames (nests, concepts) of a given field that exists in the mind in the native language.

It is necessary to distinguish between the causes and factors of the speech realization of the derived meanings of anthropomorphic lexemes in speech. First of all, the personal factor acts as the main reason in the speech expression of derived meanings. After all, any speech reality occurs on the basis of the communicative goal of a person. The communicative goal as a primary phenomenon determines the structure of speech, the selection and use of language units. The level of clarity and perseverance of the speaker's goal is determined, on the one hand, by his stable qualities, such as worldview, cultural and moral level, taste, principles of activity, character, will, and, on the other hand, by unstable states, such as his mood, health and time. Also, external factors have an impact on internal factors that achieve such a goal.

The communicative goal can be clear or vague, strict or opposite to it. When setting a clear and understandable goal, the figurative meanings of language units occupy a special place. As already mentioned, the communicative goal is to receive or transmit information, and with a weak intention of influence, there is practically no manifestation of metaphorical meanings in speech, or even when observed, these derived meanings are linguisticized, i.e. , they are characterized by a rather low level of influence on the feelings of the communicator.[129] This situation in itself leads to a decrease in the role of external factors. This can be seen in academic or official texts.

Examples of texts with limited use of metaphorical meanings of words: 1. Why do words and terms from other languages change? First, there has never been and never will be a pure language in the world that has not acquired words from another language. This statement also applies to the terminological systems of the language. The word was appropriated for the reason that political, economic and cultural relations between peoples require, and the specific reasons for the language open the way to this (R. Donierov, "Some questions of the terminology of the Uzbek language"). 2. The porous shell surrounding Keren is also called meson shell, meson cloud or meson "skin". The nucleon is surrounded by a cloud of pi mesons, which are constantly generated and absorbed. More precisely, the nucleus

---

[129] Maltsev V.A. Emotion and the meaning of the word // Abstracts of reports of the Minsk State Pedagogical Institute of Foreign Languages. 15th session. - Minsk, 1963, -S.43.

together with the pi meson cloud forms a nucleon. The cloud of pi mesons is positively charged in the proton. However, in addition to positive pi-mesons in the proton, of course, there must also be a neutral pi-criterion cloud. The meson shell of the neutron contains both positive and negative pi-mesons. It also has neutral pi mesons. Therefore, in a cloud of "pure" pi-mesons, the electric and nuclear dimensions of the nucleon should be the same, but experiments have shown that these dimensions are somewhat different from each other. Theorists resolved this contradiction by assuming that, in addition to the pion cloud, there are two more unknown neutral mesons heavier than the pion. (R.Bekjonov, "Nuclear Physics", T.: Uchitel, 1975. - P.71-75) Theorists resolved this contradiction by assuming that in addition to the pion cloud there are two more unknown neutral mesons heavier than the pi-meson. (R. Bekjonov, "Nuclear Physics", T .: Uchitel, 1975. - S. 71-75) Theorists resolved this contradiction by assuming that, in addition to the pion cloud, there are two more unknown neutral mesons heavier than the pion. (R. Bekjonov, "Nuclear Physics", T .: Uchitel, 1975. - P. 71-75)

Texts where the use of metaphorical meanings of words is not limited: 1. According to the requirements of this law, people should be kind to each other, especially harmony between relatives, kindness *Question It is necessary to judge, to show respect to the dead, to show respect to the living, one of the main conditions of this law: each person must bury the body of the deceased. As long as that's the case, isn't it your sister's most sacred duty to leave her brother's body on the bosom of the earth?!*

Will not the failure to fulfill this duty be a departure from the sacred laws imposed on the human conscience by the living gods, fearing the judgment of mortal servants?(A. Alimukhamedov, "History of Ancient Literature") 2.*So, the resonance, which exists for a short time, is it a simple combination of -xi minus hyperon and Pi-meson, which has not lost its individual properties, or is it a particle called O during this time? Or, in such a short space of time, for the concept of particle and compound, this implied difference has no meaning? Science still cannot answer these questions.* (R. Bekjonov, "Nuclear Physics"). 3.*Was it not a satirical blade of the writer, the bearer of ugly habits that poisoned the prosperous life of Otabek and Kumushbibi, who expressed true human love based on an important ideological and aesthetic concept in Otgan Kunlar?* "Although my Uzbek mother was chubby, she was famous for her sharpness towards her husband"description of the tribe, the presence of contradictions between the weaknesses of its inner world and the claims of its external actions*IIsn't this an internal funny conflict characteristic of satirical images? In my opinion, the Uzbek mother is literally embodied as a literary and satirical image.*("Uzbek language and literature")

It should be noted that the use of metaphorical derived meanings in scientific texts depends on two situations:

1) the use of metaphorical meanings depending on the nature of the field;

2) the use of metaphorical meanings depending on the nature of the communicator.

In the fields of specific sciences, in comparison with natural, especially biological, metaphorical meanings of words are relatively rare, while literary sciences study fiction in which figurative figurative meanings are effectively used, and metaphorical meanings are much more common. .

Anthropocentric metaphors are effectively used in scientific texts for a clear and memorable transmission of thoughts, despite the unfavorable pragmatic situation: 1. These two substances differ from each other in their chemical properties: having a local effect, they control vascular tone and capillary permeability is a regulatory hormone (see . chapter XVIII), and angiotensin 1 is physiologically neutral (see chapter XIV). (A. Ya. Nikolaev. Biology, chemistry. - Tashkent: Ibn Sina, 199.1. - P. 15.) 2. Sets of rational and irrational numbers together form a set of real numbers. (V.K. Gabulov, Functional analysis and computational mathematics. - Tashkent: Uchitel, 1976. p. 206) 3. Here, since $a0 = -3$ $a3 = 2$, based on our statement, the image of the root is $+1$, -1 , $+$ be equal to one of the numbers 3, -3, The denominator b can take only one of the values $+1$, -1, $+2$, -2. (V.K. Gabulov That work, p. 27)

Anthropomorphic metaphors are actively used in scientific texts; in general, the enrichment and development of metaphors depends on literary texts, in particular, on the ability of creators to create new expressions. In this sense, when determining the specifics of anthropomorphic metaphors, an analysis of literary, especially poetic, texts gives a good result.

Socio-pragmatic and gender characteristics of anthropomorphic metaphors in literary texts. In more recent studies, a number of types of meaning transfer have been identified. Including metonymy, synecdoche, sarcasm, irony. However, in Uzbek linguistics, scientific research to identify specific types of metaphors was carried out and this process continues. In particular, metaphors began to be studied anthropocentrically. In scientific studies, it has been divided into a number of types such as zoomorphic, phytomorphic, anthropomorphic. Due to the lack of scientific research on the specific study of anthropomorphic metaphors, only the figurative use of parts of the human body is considered as an anthropomorphic metaphor. Linguistic, socio-pragmatic relationship that occurs when all things that belong to a person and are inherent only to him, in particular, all parts of the body, actions, situations, experiences, feelings, are transferred to other objects, *kulfat* **through** *a thousand times. /The tower that faced ruthless stone-throwing, vulture, / humiliation!/*And here, when the minaret is described as a national, spiritual value of the people, as the past, historical memory, the ancestor of society, the author tries to bring it to life, to express it at the level of a person. "going to kulfat" is characteristic of members of society - people, and not a minaret. In the following verses we can also see the expression of human behavior and situations:

He woke up in the morning shouting: / I am a weed, a wet weed. / I am a weed, many-leaved, / when I grow into a pumpkin. /I'm a weed if I jump/ I can swing like a tree. / I will shout to the bird, / If I get cured... / That night the sky heard the sound of a gentle song.(Elections. Shavkat Rahman, 23 years old.)

The verbs "grow up", "shout", "hear" used in the text of the poem have a figurative meaning, since they are used in relation to things and events other than a person, and this situation creates anthropomorphic metaphors. / The East wakes up beautiful, / it is like the sunrise, / while it is in the summer heat, / while it looks at the world in a dream.

The highlighted words are also mostly personal and are applied to space depending on the context. In the following sentences, contrary to the lexical meanings of the first sentence, it is expressed in the form "The East sleeps beautifully": At one end of the broken world / The East is beautiful **sleeping**, / like butter - *even though they bury it, / all the same, the soul will grow, the mind will grow. / But from sleep wake up beautiful amazement covers everything. / The East* *is a place awakened like the sun / **feel the world are you still sleeping**...* (Elections. Sh. Rahman, 27.)

In the poetic text, actions and situations characteristic of women are transferred to other events. In particular, it is noticeable that the verbs "smile" and "tie", as well as the lexemes included in the group of nouns "hair", have moved from the semantic meaning that they always fulfill to a different stylistic, pragmatic meaning: ***got rich.***/

Anthropomorphic metaphors can be divided into the following types according to certain similarities:

1. Anthropomorphic metaphors with similarity of form
2. Anthropomorphic metaphors with similarities of characters
3. Anthropomorphic metaphors with similarity of action
4. Anthropomorphic metaphors with situation analogy

Anthropomorphic metaphors also have gender characteristics. In poetic texts, authors often use forms, signs and actions characteristic of women when they express things, objects, events that are different from people. For example, Shavkat Rahman tries to express the events of life in his poems mainly as follows: / I observed - each planet is the color of an apple, /***hanging in ur shabbodas,*** /*Ankhor is heard and flows - / The curtain sways in the wind.* /

In these verses, "to swing" and "to swing" are actions characteristic of women. Here the author uses this verb to refer to an apple. Although people in society use common language units in the process of communication, some language units differ by gender. In particular, words such as "kiss", "flirt", "flirt", "hayo", "for" are typical for women. In the Uzbek language, a woman is metaphorically compared to a flower. However, in the artistic text, there are places where the inner feelings and state of mind of a woman are expressed in the image of a flower: / In a courtyard surrounded by walls, / A girl *leaning on the mouth of a stream, / A rose **average** Who is in love / trembles at the thought of it. /*

The meaning of the verb "middle" used in one of the verses can be understood, since the text refers to a person through a flower, which is not characteristic of other creatures. However, according to the poetic attitude of the landscape, it is also possible that we are talking about the flower itself, that it is neglected. / Oh, I tell you, the rose is bad ***trembled**/ I asked if the fragrances were spilled. / In the oil of the shining wall / My broken heart trembles gently. / Such a flower ... in a deserted courtyard, / Trembles so much from someone else's gaze. / Pearls in whose love, / opened at the top, / Bye...*/

The adjective "hokisor" used in the following sentence expresses a characteristic of people. But in this context it applies to a flower. The mental state verb "tremble" can be used both between people and with other things, but it refers to an action, not a state. The expression in this text means a situation, therefore, in the verse "trembling from someone else's gaze, this verb is a metaphorical transfer of meaning." / Such a flower... you are still modest, / after all, if you hide your pain, / oh salinity, the sun is still cruel, / velvet leaves always fall. / (Sh.R. "Someone's flower")

One of the most common types of anthropomorphic metaphors are situational metaphors. It is known that the combination "shameless babmak" used in the text is typical only for a person. Its use in relation to a flower, as well as the combination of "hiding pain" in the next couplet in the style of "if he hides, then I will hide" is a clear example of conveying meaning based on analogy.

The night falls, the ancient silent night, /

moon and clouds- *All of them, /*

with countless dark shields/

trees hide fruits. /

A piece of the universe on earth - in the garden, /

starts to break, sudden silence, incessant rains... Drops colorful apples until dawn/night. (Selection. Sh. Rahmon "Kiyas") The transfer of human actions to other objects and events serves to increase the effectiveness of not only poetic, but also prose, journalistic texts. However, its expression in a poetic context differs sharply from others. For example, in the paragraph above "trees hide *fruits*In the stanza, the verbs "hide" or "play" and "shoot" in the last stanza express action. The important point is that these verbs form a metaphor because they are used in relation to the night. In the following poem, Shavkat Rahman creates a series of metaphors to express the situation: In a meadow of mint, / He frolicked like a peacock, / I looked into his sun-dazzled blue eyes / With my crazy eyes, / then I started kissing: every time I kissed, this dog giggled and laughed. (Sh. Rahman. "Kholat") that along with anthropomorphic metaphors, zoomorphic metaphors are also used in this context.Vwe can see.

When the author describes the water in his heart, he depicts it both with human qualities and with symbols of birds, which are symbols of beauty. All visual means are based on an almost figurative meaning. In literary criticism, the transfer of human characteristics to other inanimate objects and animals is also called animation. From a linguistic point of view, such events are called metaphors. Among them, anthropomorphic metaphors of scientific language are characteristic of man: From the cold depths of the Universe / They received news from us, / They wandered in endless space / Forever remained on the blind earth ...

In literary criticism, there are artistic descriptive means known as animation and narration. In them, the behavior characteristic of a person, as well as the transfer of speech to other things and events, is called diagnostics. According to linguistic rules, this is a metaphor in a general sense. ThenGIn studies of the first period, a number of types of meaning transfer were distinguished. Including metonymy, synecdoche, sarcasm, irony. However, in Uzbek linguistics, scientific research to identify specific types of metaphors was carried out and this process continues. In particular, metaphors began to be studied anthropocentrically. In scientific studies, it has been divided into a number of types such as zoomorphic, phytomorphic, anthropomorphic. Due to the lack of scientific research on the specific study of anthropomorphic metaphors, only the figurative use of parts of the human body is considered as an anthropomorphic metaphor. Linguistic, socio-pragmatic relationship that occurs when all things that belong to a person and are inherent only to him, in particular, all parts of the body, actions, situations, experiences, feelings, are transferred to other objects, *Say hello, / but why leave the earth in darkness / and put on bring it back?/ Why can't you stay here forever/ Why will you leave when you're forgotten?/ Will you find less value in our dark hearts?*(Sh. Rahman. "Nur")

In order to figuratively depict light, the poet expresses it on the basis of human behavior. As you know, light does not travel. U to characteristic actions are completely different, for example, to shine, even to spread, to fall, refer to other phenomena and are applied to light in a figurative or metaphorical sense.

Or you don't see the truth at all, / or you don't see religion, pride, / maybe you can't stay forever, / maybe because returns light (Sh. Rahman. "Nur")

In addition to poetic texts, there are also rare examples of anthropomorphic metaphors in prose contexts. In this case, one can observe migration events involving more parts of the human body: *It was the beginning of autumn days and the beginning of winter days. The yellow leaves on the trees have fallen, ground surface its winter is yellow **wear his clothes** even these cherry trees, which saved their leaves from falling in the shade on four sides, could not stand the black cold of the night and with the slightest movement of the hand tore the leaves from them shirt by shirt. It's clear and the sun is up, but on this day it doesn't matter much, it's a black cold sun force it was cut in ini./*(A. Kadiri "Past Days")

Kumushbibi appeared from the middle door. The fullness of his nose disappeared and he lost weight, but this thinness does not detract from his beauty, but rather lifts his wrists. Onion eyebrows flutter **show your self** when you fall a little, beautiful eyes are always dark and bright **profession** were a collar made of Soviet fur, which he wore today from the cold, aroused envy in people, and elegant frogs **kiss** However, there seemed to be a flaw in it: Shahla did not play with her nose with her eyes, and then moved with some heaviness in the check. / (A. Kadiri "Past Days")

The interaction of isolated phrases acquires a specific social and pragmatic meaning. In any case, this meaning did not arise directly, but through the transfer of meaning. Although the lexeme "earn" is actually specific to people, it is also used in the context of other events. Or maybe the author describes the author's touch in such terms as "kissing" graceful skin frogs. Such an expression was chosen to arouse the jealousy of the reader.

In our opinion, in the process of beginning to understand the environment and existence, humanity relied on parts of its body, its actions and characteristics when naming or expressing things outside of itself. In particular, anthropomorphic metaphors can be seen in the following verses: / No sound... No sound! / No pain, no hardships... / Words rise like statues from stone shoulders. / Silent graves lie with their mouths open, / Like a memory of devastated lands. /

Literary texts can reveal the full potential of anthropomorphic metaphors. This possibility is relatively limited in journalistic, scientific and socio-political texts, but it should be emphasized that a purely scientific text is not understandable to members of society, even scientists can clearly express their scientific results through anthropomorphic or other types of metaphors. It should be noted here that the issue of using metaphors in political texts should also be scientifically studied.

TABLE OF CONTENTS

FORMATION OF THE SCIENCE ABOUT THE LANGUAGE OF THE TEXT AND THE STUDY OF METAPHORS ....

The study of metaphor in world linguistics..........................

The study of metaphor in Uzbek linguistics............................

The study of metaphors in text and discourse....................................

MEANS OF CONNECTING THE TEXT AND ITS PARTS ....

Phonetic features of the text ....

Lexico-semantic features of the text ....

Morphological features of the text ....

Syntactic features of the text ....

Migrations and their sociolinguistic features ....

PRINCIPLES OF ANALYSIS OF DIFFERENT STYLES OF TEXTS.....

Representation of metaphor in a literary text ....

Representation of metaphors in journalistic texts ....

Analysis of linguistic means in texts of scientific style ....

LINKS USED

1. Mirziyoev Sh.M. We will build a free and prosperous, democratic state of Uzbekistan together // Speech at a joint meeting of the chambers of the Oliy Majlis, dedicated to the ceremony of inauguration of the President of the Republic of Uzbekistan. - Tashkent.: Uzbekistan, 2016. - 56 p.

2. Mirziyoev Sh.M. We will build our great future together with our brave and noble people. - Tashkent.: Uzbekistan, 2017. - 488 p.

3. Mirziyoev Sh.M. Critical analysis, strict discipline and personal responsibility should be the daily rule of every leader. - Tashkent.: Uzbekistan, 2017. - 104 p.

4. Decree No. PF-4947 of the President of the Republic of Uzbekistan "On the Strategy of Actions for the Further Development of the Republic of Uzbekistan" // Narodnoe Slovo. February 8, 2017 #28

5. Decree of the President of the Republic of Uzbekistan "On improving the efficiency of spiritual and educational work and raising the development of the sphere to a new level." // People's Word, July 29, 2017. #132

6. Decree of the President of the Republic of Uzbekistan dated October 21, 2019 No. PF-5850 "On measures to radically increase the prestige and position of the Uzbek language as the state language" // Khalk Sozi, October 22, 2019 #218

7. Khodjiev A. Actual problems of Uzbek linguistics // Uzbek language and literature. 2006, No. 3. S. 26-30; No. 5. - B.30-39.

8. Ibragimova R.S. Linguistic study of the concept WOMAN in French and Uzbek: Philol. Ph.D.... dis.author. - Tashkent, 2012. - 25 p.

9. Yuldoshev M., Isakov Z., Heydarov Sh. Linguistic analysis of a literary text. - Tashkent: Publishing House of the National Library of Uzbekistan. A. Navoi, 2010.

10. Yuldoshev M. Linguo-poetics of a literary text. - Tashkent: Science, 2008.

11. Yuldoshev M., Yadgarov K. Organization of practical classes on linguistic analysis of a literary text. - Tashkent: TDPU them. Nizomi, 2007.

12. Lapasov Yu. Artistic text and linguistic analysis. - Tashkent: Teacher, 1995.

13. Gilichev E. Linguistic analysis of the text. - Bukhara: Bukhara University, 2000.

14. Maslova V. A. Introduction to language culture. - M., 1997. - 208 p.

15. Maslova V.A. Language culture. Textbook for students of higher educational institutions. - M .: "Academy", 2001. - 204 p.

16. Makhmudov N. Comparisons - a product of figurative thinking // Uzbek language and literature. - Tashkent, 2011. - No. 3. - B. 23-27.

17. Makhmudov N. In search of ways of perfect language learning... // Uzbek language and literature. - Tashkent, 2012. - No. 5. - B. 3-16.

18. Makhmudov N., Khudoyberganova D. Explanatory Dictionary of Comparisons of the Uzbek Language. - Tashkent: Ma'naviyat, 2013. - 320 p.

19. Mirtozhiev M. Semasiology of the Uzbek language. - Tashkent: Mumtoz soz, 2010. - 284 p.

20. Musaev K. Fundamentals of the theory of translation. Textbook. - Tashkent: Nauka, 2005. - 352 p.

21. Nurmonov A., Makhmudov N., Akhmedov A., Solikhodzhaeva S. Meaningful syntax of the Uzbek language. - Tashkent.: Nauka, 1992. - 233 p.

22. Bushui A.M. language and reality. - Samarkand: SamGIIA. 2005.

23. Olshansky I. G. Linguistics and culture: Methodological foundations and basic concepts // Language and Culture. - Issue. 2. - M., 1999.

24. Petrenko O. A. Ethnic mentality and folklore. - Kursk, 1996. - 216 p.

25. Potebnya A.A. Symbol and myth and national culture. - M., 2000. - 480 p.

26. Slyshkin G.G. The word k is the character of the text. Linguistic and cultural concepts of precedent texts in the consciousness of discourse. - M.: Publishing center "Academy", 2000. - 139 p.

27. Safarov Sh. Principles of system-semantic analysis of syntax. - Tashkent.: Tashkent settlement. ped. i-t, 1983. - 97 p.

28. Safarov Sh. Semantics. - T.: Our own state science. ed., 2013. - 344 p.

29. Usmanova Sh. The role of gaps in intercultural communication // Linguist. Collection of scientific articles. V. - Tashkent: "Akademnashr", 2013. -B 152-156.

30. Sorokin Yu.A. Ethnopsycholinguistics. - M.: Nauka, 1988. - 192 p.

31. Bozorov O. Assessment in Uzbek. - Tashkent: Science. 1995. - 132 p.

32. Teliya V.N. Russian phraseology: semantic, pragmatic and linguoculturological aspects. - M.: School "Languages of Russian culture", 1996. - 288 p.

33. Toporov V. N. Mif. Ritual. Symbol. Image: Studies in the field of mythopoetic. - M., 1995. - 624 p.

34. Khudoyberganova D. Anthropocentric study of the text. - Tashkent: Science, 2013.

35. Khudaiberganova D.S. Anthropocentric interpretation of artistic texts in the Uzbek language. Doctoral diss. abstract. - Tashkent., 2015. - 102 p.

36. Yusupov O'.K. On the meaning of terms, concept, concept and linguistic culture // Stylistics in modern directions of linguistics. - T., 2011. - B. 49-55.

37. Shaklein V.M. Language culture. Tradition and innovation. - M., 2012. - 301 p.

38. Eshankulov J. Folklore: Image and Interpretation. - Against: Nasaf, 1999. - 104 p.

39. Usmanova Sh. National and cultural features of Uzbek and Korean non-verbal communication // International Journal of Central Asian Studies. Volume. IX. - Seoul, 2004. -B. 48-60.

40. Makhmaraimova Sh. T. Language culture. - Tashkent: Cholpon, 2017. - 164 p.

41. Mominov S. Sociolinguistic features of communicative behavior of Uzbeks. DDA-T.: 2000. - 50 p.

42. Salieva Z.I. Conceptual Significance and National-Cultural Specificity of the Sentence in the English and Uzbek Languages: Author's abstract of diss. - Tashkent, 2010. - 24 p.

43. Negmatov Kh., Bozorov O. Language and speech. - T.: 1993.

44. Ergasheva M.V. Linguistic landscape of the universe and its division into semantic fields / M.V. Ergasheva.– Text: // Young scientist. - 2016. - No. 3.1 (107.1). - S. 59-62.

45. Iskandarova Sh. Learning the vocabulary of the Uzbek language based on the content area. Doctor of Philology... author.- Tashkent., 1999. - 48 rubles.

46. Sobirov A. Studying the lexical level of the Uzbek language based on the principle of a system of systems.- Tashkent: Ma'naviyat, 2004. - 232 p.

47. Mominov S. Characteristics of the communicative behavior of Uzbeks in the gender aspect // Uzbek language and literature, 1999, no. 5 - B. 64-66.

48. Mominov S., Rasulov K. On the social role of communicants and speech communication // Actual problems of stylistics and phraseology. - Samarkand: SamDU, 2007. - S.70-72.

49. Muslimonova N.R. Categorical, adjuvant and accompanying meaning in grammatical forms (on the example of tense and mood categories). NDA, - Tashkent, 2007. - 25 p.

50. Nabieva D. The manifestation of dialectical categories at the levels of the Uzbek language (on the basis of generality and specificity). Philol. Candidate's dissertation …… abstract. - Tashkent:, 2007. - 46 p.

51. Negmatov H., Vohidova N., Toirova G. From structural linguistics to pragmalinguistics // Foreign Philology, 2007, No. 4. - B.38-41

52. Nurmonov A., Yuldoshev B. Linguistics and natural sciences. - Tashkent: Shark, 2001. - 160 p.

53. Nurmonov A., Makhmudov N., Akhmedov A., Solikhodjaeva S. Meaningful syntax of the Uzbek language. - Tashkent: Nauka, 1992. - 234 p.

54. Nurmonov A., Khakimov M. Theoretical formation of language pragmatics // Uzbek language and literature, 2001, No. 4. - P.54-58.

55. Rasulov R. General linguistics. - Tashkent.: Publishing house of science and technology, 2007. - 256 p.

Printed in the USA
CPSIA information can be obtained
at www.ICGtesting.com
LVHW082154030424
776152LV00009B/205